DESIGN CONTROL
TOWARDS A NEW APPROACH

◊

DESIGN CONTROL
TOWARDS A NEW APPROACH

A. C. Hall

Butterworth Architecture
An imprint of Butterworth-Heinemann Ltd
Linacre House, Jordan Hill, Oxford OX2 8DP

 A member of the Reed Elsevier plc group

OXFORD   LONDON   BOSTON
NEW DELHI   SINGAPORE   SYDNEY
TOKYO   TORONTO   WELLINGTON

First published 1996

British Library Cataloguing in Publication Data
A catalogue record for this book is available from the British
Library

ISBN 0 7506 2390 X

Library of Congress Cataloguing in Publication Data
A catalogue record for this book is available from the Library of
Congress

Typeset by Scribe Design, Gillingham, Kent
Printed and bound in Great Britain

CONTENTS

ACKNOWLEDGEMENTS

Thanks are due especially to James Doe of Dacorum Borough Council for his collaboration and confidence in the ideas and to Professor Jeremy Whitehand of Birmingham University for his helpful suggestions throughout. Alan Stones of Essex County Council made many important comments and suggestions and my research student, Richard Mabbitt, contributed important material to Chapter 4. The co-operation of the staff of the planning departments of Chelmsford, Chiltern, Dacorum, Redbridge, Richmond-upon-Thames, Sutton and Wycombe Councils is gratefully acknowledged. I am also grateful for the use of the design guide collection at the School of Planning at the University of Central England. Essential assistance with the photography was provided by my colleague Tony Ashton and with the drawings by Ian Crawford and David Holdsworth. The majority of the computer images in Chapter 6 were produced by my research assistants William Colchester and Dominic McGrath. Finally, this book would not have been possible had I not spent a very influential sabbatical year at the Joint Centre for Urban Design at Oxford Brookes University.

SOURCE OF FIGURES

Figures 3.2, 3.4–3.6, 4.4, 4.5e, 4.7, 4.8c, 4.10, 4.11, 4.12, 4.13, 4.16 and 6.3c photographs by Tony Ashton.

Figures 3.1, 3.7a, 3.7c, and 3.8 are reproduced by permission of Essex County Council.

Figures 3.3, 4.3, 4.6, 4.9, 4.19–4.22, 5.4–5.7, 5.9, 5.13, 5.14, 5.17, 5.20 and 5.23 are reproduced from the Ordnance Survey, Crown Copyright reserved.

Figure 3.7b is reproduced by permission of Leeds City Council.

Figures 4.1 and 4.2 are reproduced by permission of G.I. Barnett & Son Ltd, Dagenham.

Figures 4.5a–d, 4.8a,f, 4.14, 4.17 and 4.18 were redrawn and styled by Ian Crawford from original sketches by the author.

Figures 4.8b,d,e, and 4.15 were redrawn and styled by David Holdsworth from original sketches by the author.

Figures 4.19–4.22 are reproduced by permission of the Essex Chronicle Series.

Figures 5.1 and 5.9–5.12 are reproduced by permission of the London Borough of Richmond-upon-Thames.

Figures 5.2 and 5.3 are reproduced by permission of the London Borough of Redbridge.

Figures 5.4–5.8 are reproduced by permission of the London Borough of Sutton.

Figures 5.13, 5.14 and 5.15 are reproduced by permission of Chiltern District Council.

Figure 5.16 is reproduced by permission of Wycombe District Council.

Figures 5.17–5.23 are reproduced by permission of Dacorum Borough Council.

Figures 5.24–5.27 are reproduced by permission of Cambridgeshire County Council.

Figures 5.28 and 5.29 are reproduced by permission of Newbury District Council.

Figure 6.1 was produced by Dominic McGrath under the direction of the author.

Figure 6.2 was produced by William Colchester under the direction of the author.

Figures 6.2b–d are reproduced by permission of Wilby and Burnett, Saffron Walden.

Figure 6.3 (local plan content) is reproduced by permission of Chelmsford Borough Council.

Figure 6.4 was produced by Dr Alan Day of the University of Bath.

Table 3.1 is reproduced by permission of Professor John Punter of the University College of Cardiff.

INTRODUCTION

This book addresses the ability of planning agencies to control the design of town and country. It does not seek to define or explore the concept of **good design**, important as this is. Rather, it examines the means by which these agencies pursue the control of design and, in doing so, focuses upon how policies are generated and how they are put over to others.

Design control requires negotiation between several parties of which the planning agency is but one. Its aim should be the benefit of the public at large. Clarity of purpose and the provision of ample information at an early stage should be its watchwords. Unfortunately, neither of these qualities has been much in evidence. There has been a paucity of statements of the intentions of planning agencies. General guidance has been forthcoming in some cases but little information on deliberate policy. This is not because there has been little intervention by planning authorities or because their actions betray little content to their policy. On the contrary, they do impose their views and local people demand action from them. The impression gained is that the policies exist largely in the mind of the officials concerned rather than in the public realm. This can place both potential developers and the general public at a significant disadvantage. There can be two reasons for this state of affairs. One is an unhealthy one: to protect one's views from challenge. Whether or not this is the case, it will not be pursued here. A more legitimate reason is the lack of a proper method, in particular an agreed language, for setting down design policies. Although there has been progress towards this over the years, notably in townscape studies, there remains much to be done. How to make good this deficiency is the issue addressed here.

The book sets out practical proposals, some, such as the **design area**, entirely original. They may appear quite simple at first sight but this does not prevent them being powerful. If they are so simple then why are they not already in use? The proposals made here are only the first step in a new direction. Many more books by many more authors will, hopefully, follow for much work remains to be done. For the moment, the reader is asked to consider the arguments for a new approach to design control.

The origin of the enquiry

The subject of this book arose in the mid 1980s when the author was studying ways of improving parts of his local town. This exercise brought home just how little information was available on the policies of British planning authorities for the design of parts of towns. Although a local land-use plan was available for the areas studied, it gave little guidance on matters of urban design. It was not that the planning authority did not intervene in such issues: it certainly did. It was not that amenity groups, businesses and the public at large were not concerned with design issues: they certainly were. What was clear was that there was a gap, and a large one at that, in the development plan provision.

The thinking moved on to what this policy provision would look like if it did exist. The idea emerged that it would need to be based on small areas. These **design areas** would not be pre-set but would vary according to the policy context. It then appeared that this rather simple idea had considerable power. It would facilitate policy for features such as roads, which were normally to be found on land-use boundaries and not seen as design elements in their own right. It would also facilitate variation in the intensity of planning control from area to area, something that had been a recurring issue within British planning practice. It also became clear that such design areas should cover all parts of a town, not just those where redevelopment was imminent or which were of a particularly sensitive nature. Much of the change in existing urban areas is of an incremental nature and can cause the quality of the environment in, say, outlying residential areas to improve or deteriorate. Policies towards such areas should be made clear even if they were largely of a 'hands-off' nature.

The next question was what should be the nature of the policy statements within the design areas? It was noted that urban design, and planning generally, involved negotiation between at least two, often several, parties. Negotiation would be assisted if a distinction could be made between the intentions of the parties and the possible design outcomes. It followed that it was the planning authority's **objectives** that should be made clear for each design area. These ideas were developed further and a case study of Chelmsford was prepared. The results were published as articles and a short book.[1]

Further work was then undertaken to develop the methodology more fully. The relationship between goals and objectives was improved and the distinction between intentions and outcomes elaborated into a **four-way split**: the objectives, criteria for their achievement, material advising on how they might be achieved, and control procedures leading to their implementation. The Chelmsford case study was developed further and examples of points of correspondence with current British practice were sought. Proper note was also taken of current practice in Europe and North America. This work was paralleled throughout by an investigation into the application of computer visualization to design control. The ability of computers to generate realistic colour pictures of proposed development which can then be altered interactively can enable lay people to participate fully in the design control process. Finally the work all came together as this book.

The content and aim

The first two chapters establish the need for design control as a legitimate planning operation. They identify the lack of policy statements in current practice and the consequent problems experienced by both participants in the development process and the public at large. Theoretical and historical perspectives are reviewed. Chapter 3 develops a new methodology aimed at the production of effective design plans. Distinctions are made between design goals, design objectives, performance criteria, advisory material and control procedures and means of generating them are proposed. The concept of the **design area** is introduced and its application to varying the intensity of development control is explored. The development of standard forms of objective and their implications are discussed. Chapter 4 provides an illustration of the application of the ideas proposed by means of a case study of the town of Chelmsford. Chapter 5 draws attention to the relationship between the ideas suggested and examples from British practice. Special reference is made to the Dacorum Borough Council *Residential Character Study*, which utilized many of the proposals. Chapter 6 notes the problem of communicating design control policies to the lay public, reviews the media available and advocates the use of computer visualization as the way forward. It suggests that, in the long term, a computer-based multimedia approach should provide the vehicle for the interactive and responsive development plan.

The discussion draws upon examples from recent practice. Although space is devoted to the experiences of design control in Western Europe and North America, practicality has dictated a reliance on British practice. The proposals should not, however, be read solely within the confines of current British planning legislation and government requirements. They are aimed at all government systems where design is a matter of negotiation involving public bodies. They may, in some cases, conflict with details of current British procedures. However, British procedures, as in other countries, are subject to frequent alteration and the arguments of this book are intended to influence changes in the long term.

The people who will read the argument and, hopefully, act upon the recommendations will largely be practising professionals in the fields of town and country planning, urban design, architecture, surveying and others concerned with the development process. They should see the proposals as an important step forward in planning methodology. There has been a lack of policy statements for design guidance, in large part for want of an accessible method for preparing them. This book provides this link and, as such, should be of use to a wide range of professionals. The book will also be of interest to academics not only in the professional fields mentioned but also in geography and urban studies. Geographers will be interested in the approach taken to urban morphology and the ways in which practical applications have been found for this area of academic study. However, the most important beneficiaries of the proposals will be those who may not form the majority of the readership, the public at large. Implicit in the reasoning is the principle that the lay public should be able to participate in the discussion of the design of the areas in which they live and work. Clearly accessible policies should empower them and give them an effective role in negotiations.

The aim of the work is the improvement of planning practice. It does not by any means represent the final word on the subject but, on the contrary, it is hoped it will be the beginning of a process that will result in more effective design control. Although it is intended for direct use in practice, it will have been successful if it merely stimulates fruitful experimentation and debate.

Notes and references

1. A. C. Hall (1990) *Generation of Objectives for Design Control*, Chelmsford: Anglia College Enterprises. The articles were: Hall (1990) Generating design objectives for local areas: a methodology and case study application to Chelmsford, Essex. *Town Planning Review*, 61(3), 287–309; Hall A. C. (1990) Design control – a call for a new approach. *The Planner*, 76(39), 14–18; and Hall A. C. (1992) Letting the public in on design control. *Town and Country Planning*, 61(3), 83–5.

Chapter 1

THE NEED FOR DESIGN POLICY

The necessity for design control

The starting point for the argument of this book is that design control exists as a political fact and is a feature of government (at least in developed countries) that is unlikely to go away. Since the late nineteenth century there has been concern among certain vocal sections of the public about the quality of their immediate physical environment, as used, inhabited and enjoyed by themselves. This concern has figured prominently in the development of town and country planning and the ideas that have sustained it. All people use buildings and the spaces between them and their arrangement and appearance have an effect on both the functioning of people's daily lives and their aesthetic pleasure. It would, indeed, be surprising in a sophisticated society if there was not some public concern for quality in these matters and a desire that the machinery of government should, in some way, attempt to ensure that this quality is maintained. Where town and country planning systems exist their outcomes in the shape of settlements and landscapes will be the basis on which their success is judged. As Keeble[1] has pointed out:

It has often been said with truth that Planning is principally judged by the appearance of development that has received planning permission.

But surely, many will say, design control has been a matter of great controversy with the architecture and planning professions frequently at loggerheads and governments showing apathy, and sometimes hostility, towards the whole idea. It is not the purpose of this book to recount a history of design control as this is done well elsewhere[2] but it must be said that such

history does indeed demonstrate much conflict. However, it is difficult to find, even among its most trenchant critics anyone who argues that the quality of the physical environment is either of no importance or that quality can be maintained with no intervention by anyone at any time nor in any place. Rather, the controversy turns on how the control should be handled. Who should intervene, to what degree and in what sort of localities? Have past methods achieved the desired results and what approaches should be used in the future? It can be argued that 'bad design' is in no-one's interest. Builders wish to sell their products, architects seek reputations and commissions, and planners are under local political pressure to please the public. The arguments are not about the need for quality or about the need for some kind of intervention but rather about the methods employed and the exact nature of the 'design' that is being controlled.

Much heat is generated on topics that are not really central to urban design. Many of the most acerbic architectural critics[3] maintain the momentum of their argument by concentrating on the aesthetic and stylistic aspects (which are, in their view, matters for the architect) and neglecting the functional content of urban design. Design quality is seen by them as a subjective matter. That there could be aspects of design which could be judged against objective functional criteria is not mentioned. Can it be believed that they would make the same argument for the internal layout of buildings? The public makes use of the spaces between buildings in much the same way as they do their interiors and they have important functional requirements that need to be taken into account.

The fallacy underlying the more extreme aspects of the debate on design control is that it is not

1

fundamentally a 'for and against' issue (except for anyone advocating that quality in design is totally unimportant). If quality is important for the design of settlements, in both functional and aesthetic terms, then it is legitimate to debate how this quality should be defined and how it should be achieved. The answer is likely to be complex in both cases. Many individuals and organizations have an interest in the design and use of settlements but it cannot be solely a matter for particular individuals. Quality in the context of urban design is a public matter and must, therefore, be derived, wholly or partially, from the public interest and must also be a legitimate concern of local government organizations. The debate, as in other aspects of government, will turn on the balance to be struck between individual and communal interests. Whatever urban design may or not be, it is certainly a communal matter as it is concerned with the public use and enjoyment of the spaces created by buildings.

The nature of design control

If the existence of a public requirement for design control is accepted we can move on to the nature of the processes of control. To establish the context of the control process it is first necessary to establish the meaning of **urban design** as used here:

- **design** is used in the more general sense of creating form to meet an expressed need;
- its context is the outward appearance of buildings, their arrangement to form spaces, the furnishing, paving and planting of these spaces and the appearance and planting of other public open spaces;
- it is concerned with the efficient functioning of the buildings and spaces with regard to the activities of their users;
- it is concerned with the aesthetic enjoyment provided by the buildings and spaces for the same users.

It follows that the process of design must follow from statements of the needs of users and these needs will, in most cases, occur within a wider public interest. We are talking here not about a mechanical design process with fixed rules but one which evolves from a more

subjective political context. There are several theories of urban design and many views on its aim and purpose. Their appropriateness and efficacy can be judged only on the degree to which they meet the needs of what is, over time, the public interest as expressed through the political system.

The term **urban design** often conjures up visions of whole parts of towns being designed by one person. As is widely known, this rarely approximates to reality. The physical forms of settlements are determined by an incremental process. Buildings are altered, buildings are replaced, traffic circulation systems are revised, landscaping is replanted and all these changes take place not only in a piecemeal fashion but at an uneven rate. Furthermore, these changes are brought about by a development process which involves the raising of money, the acquisition of land, the design of buildings, the employment of builders and the selling or renting of the results. The experience of the large developer can apply, to a more limited extent, to the private householder who may have to find money and employ architects and builders for quite modest extensions. The design process involves many types of people and organizations, all of whom may wish to influence the final form of the development in their different ways, be they financial institutions, developers, architects, builders or the prospective users. They will all need to negotiate with each other.

Control of development is usually exercised by a local public authority, normally the appropriate tier of local government. This local authority exercises not only development control functions but may also have a direct responsibility for roads and public open spaces, all essential components of the design of settlements. There may, in some circumstances, be several local public agencies involved and possibly branches of national public authorities. The public authorities will have politicians in overall control and will be supported by professional officers. The politicians will represent different strands of opinion and be influenced, directly or indirectly, by many interest groups. Although this description of the context may seem fairly obvious, the point is that design control deals with a highly complex process in a pluralistic context. This is worth stressing as it is not always a message whose consequences are fully appreciated. It must be stated plainly here because it has significant implications for what is understood to be the nature of design control.

The meaning of control

It is important to attach the proper meaning to the word **control** when it is design control that is being discussed. Debaters of the merits of design control frequently give the impression of giving it a narrow and literal meaning and, indeed, this may be the actual understanding of many practising architects and planners. By 'narrow and literal' a simplistic model is suggested in which A exerts control by telling B exactly what to do or not to do. An applicant submits a design to a planning authority which either accepts it or rejects it according to its detailed conformity to its policy. One agency lays down to another by means of a master plan what is to be built and will brook no deviation. Whether such a narrow view was held in the past and whether some hold it today, it is certainly incompatible with the complex and pluralist nature of design control described here. Complex situations require sophisticated methods of control.

To elaborate on the last sentence requires us to revisit (with some trepidation) a controversial period in the development of planning thought when it was dominated by what was called at the time a **systems approach**. The need for caution arises from the fact that a great deal of nonsense was put about during the late 1960s and early 1970s, when this approach was in vogue. It was associated with misunderstood science and fallacious concepts to the extent that the term itself became discredited. However, most of the nonsense has passed into history and many good ideas from this period have been absorbed into planning practice. Some are now largely taken for granted to the extent that many contemporary planners may not be aware that people used to think quite differently. The fallacious path was marked by a tendency to see **systems** as absolute concepts, enjoying real existence, for which a study of process was more important than an examination of content. In particular, questions of value were not seen as crucial. This resulted from a misunderstanding of scientific method and was, ironically, nearer to obsolete views of scientific theory and to the previous planning methodology of survey–analysis–plan than it was to the new approach it was claiming to bring forth.

The correct lesson to be drawn from scientific method was that ideas arise first and are then tested against empirical data. The best writers on systems theory stressed that systems exist only in the mind of the definer and their definition must be, in the final

analysis, subjective. Such an approach applied to planning made values a starting point and led to what became known as the **rational model**. In this approach, **plans** did not have their genesis in data but in subjective **goals** which were statements of value. This had the immediate practical advantage of correspondence with the political process. As plans were required to be approved by politicians their role in the plan-making process was clarified. Furthermore, the nature of political decision-making, and the lessons learnt from the application of systems approaches to other disciplines, implied the open consideration of alternative strategies and the assessment of the degree to which they fulfilled the goals and objectives. The recognition that the development and implementation of policy was a long-term matter, that it followed a trajectory over time which should be monitored, was also valuable.

More important, however, for this discussion here were the new concepts of control that were brought in from the then comparatively new discipline of cybernetics. This was the study of control in systems drawing on biological, mechanical and electrical examples. There was a recognition that control was:

- complex;
- essential to enable the system to maintain internal stability.
- could be carried out by specialized subsystems;
- a means by which the system was steered towards desired objectives.

It was also seen not as a matter of emergency intervention by an outside agency in order to correct an unexpected malfunction but rather as a necessary part of the functioning of any complex system, including human organizations. The complex behaviour of systems could be measured in terms of the **variety** of states they could assume. The complexity of control subsystems was determined by Ashby's Law of Requisite Variety.[4]

The variety of the control device must be at least equal to that of the disturbances

In other words, complex systems require complex controls. Simple control methods could handle only simple systems.

In the biological context, control subsystems kept organisms alive and functioning. Control could be said to work by means of feedback loops. As the action of one organ affected another the organ automatically received information on the effects and readjusted its performance accordingly. By such means of control the organism would seek to maintain a state of equilibrium. (In mechanical and electronic systems such feedback arrangements could be constructed explicitly.) The biological model could be elaborated into the medical model. Human organizations could be seen as organisms that were normally self-regulating through their own internal control mechanisms. They could, by analogy, malfunction and require the intervention of an outside **medical** agency to restore them to **health**. A useful distinction can be made between internal control and that achieved by external mechanisms or agencies. It is reasonable to argue that **health** maintained by internal control is more efficient and that external intervention should be minimized. It is also significant that biological and mechanical systems are made up of subsystems that are self-regulating. They maintain their stability without continual steering by the central controls. For example, the conscious brain does not need to keep reminding the lungs and heart to keep working. Indeed, to do so would be a very inefficient method of working. Similarly inefficient would be a strictly hierarchical structure. Subsystems in living and mechanical organisms can interact directly with each other as and when appropriate. This creates a complex matrix of interactions which, while it may seem confusing to the outside observer, represents a highly efficient mode of control.

In planning we have people interacting with each other as individuals and as people grouped into agencies. They can be seen as self-regulating. These agencies in their turn interact with each other all in an attempt to influence the quality of the physical environment. Their interaction is by flows of information. The efficiency of the controls within the operation of the planning process will be linked to the efficiency of the information flows. It is the information flows that regulate power and influence between the actors in the process.

Control in planning

Models of control that take the above matters into account are useful in dealing with the pluralist context

of design control. It could be said that the general import of these views of control is now standard in planning thought and that present-day legislation and procedures by and large reflect this. However, this has not always been so and there has been an evolution to the present position. For example, it is no longer tenable to suggest that a plan can arise solely from an analysis of survey material by technical experts and that this plan could be held to represent, in a unique way, the public interest. The public interest must be seen as a wide and complex concept, particularly as far as design control decision-making is concerned. It is important in urban design decision-making as it is the counterbalance to individual interests. It is the means of balancing proposals reflecting persistent cultural values against those resulting from temporary opinions.

Over elaborate and mechanical approaches are no longer fashionable in planning methodology. The optimism of the 1950s and the 1960s was not sustained. The trends in planning thought in the mid 1970s rejected all mechanistic approaches and began to stress the pluralistic political context in which planning operated. **Advocacy planning** appeared to recognize no absolutes, only competing pressure groups, although, somewhat ironically, it re-emphasized one of the best points to come out of the systems period, and pointed out above, that planning methodology should start with value statements and consider alternatives. The more pragmatic approaches of the 1980s used what was most effective in the thinking of the previous two decades. Although the rational model was not always used explicitly, clear statements of policy that could be handled politically were the order of the day.[5]

Levels of intervention

The question of the intensity of control, that is the degree to which the planning authority should intervene, and whether this level of intervention should vary from place to place, can be a very contentious issue. It is also one that can lead to wider debates beyond the scope of this present book and, for reasons of space, it is necessary to limit the discussion. As with other aspects of design control, the debate can easily become confused as there is an interplay between more than one argument. To simplify matters, a distinction will be made between the questions of the **uniformity** of and the **general level** of intervention.

There is a particular argument for uniformity of control that is held sincerely by many people, especially architects, and it is that **good design** is an absolute concept, independent of changing public opinion and individual preferences. It is something that cannot vary over space and time and it is something that no individual or group should be denied. How it is to be achieved, however, provokes controversy among the holders of this view. Some may argue for strong intervention by professional planners at a uniformly high level. Others hold that there should be little or no intervention by planners but that quality will be ensured by the universal employment of professional architects or, alternatively, as good design sells, by leaving it to market forces. This last position is for **uniformly low level control**. It can also be advocated by people who do not hold that good design is an absolute concept but believe either that:

- only market forces deliver what people want and is what they should have, or
- individuals can determine their own aesthetic requirements without interference from public agencies.

Another argument for uniformity of intervention (and one that has been taken from time-to-time by several British planning authorities) is that it would be elitist to single out any group living in a particular part of their area for special treatment. In some cases, it would be argued, planning restrictions can increase the value of existing properties in some neighbourhoods, notably in conservation areas, and reduce them in others, so adding to an already unequal distribution of wealth.

On the other hand, there are a number of arguments for varying the degree of intervention within the plan area. The simplest, but least sophisticated, is that it is not an efficient use of scarce resources for planning staff to spread their efforts uniformly but, rather, their work should be prioritized. Most planning authorities in Britain do indeed, prioritize their efforts by type of application and there will inevitably be some spatial pattern to this. However, apart from designated priority areas such as green belts and conservation areas, spatial variation is rarely made explicit in the development plan. In particular, there is almost no evidence

of areas of low-intensity control with regard to routine residential permissions.

There are more substantial arguments available for a variable approach. Planning intervention is commonly held to be justified only if the balance between public and private interests favours the public. Officials do not intervene in, say, interior decorating or the planting of front gardens (although it is interesting to speculate if they would desist from using such powers if they possessed them). On the other hand, there is overwhelming consensus that in, say, significant historic environments the public interest requires considerable restriction on the rights of the individual. The balance between the private and communal interests will vary from place to place according to the circumstances. Such a variation exists within other aspects of land-use policy so why should it not exist for urban design issues? The answer would appear to be that it cannot when enforcement of an absolute concept of good design is adopted. If, however, this concept is not adopted, and if the idea of uniform minimum intervention is also discarded, then the variable intensity of design control emerges naturally.

Another argument for variation arises from the controversy concerning the degree to which design control (among other planning controls) inhibits commercial enterprise. Again, the balance will vary from place to place. Relaxation of controls is usually proposed for areas seeking economic regeneration. A prominent example of this has been the position adopted by the British central government during the 1980s. Circulars and planning guidance[6] encouraged a low level of intervention in design control, design being a matter for developers' understanding their market, except in 'National Parks and conservation areas'. It was also part of the government's policy for most of the 1980s that the 'burden' of interventionist development control should be lifted from industrialists seeking to establish themselves in designated priority areas.[7] The establishment of Enterprise and Simplified Planning Zones was a direct reflection of this point of view. Urban development corporations were also created to promote industrial and commercial regeneration in selected areas, with their own development control powers that enabled them to pursue their own design control policies independently of surrounding local planning authorities. Peter Hall has claimed that the origin of these policies lies in the 'non-plan' ideas of himself and others.[8] Although the

5

'non-plan' approach covers more than design control, aesthetic matters are clearly seen as part of the more detailed 'burden' which the planning system imposes and which should be relaxed.

Others may argue, however, that if there is to be variation in the intensity of control then planning is there to regulate developers and commercial concerns rather than private householders or small shopkeepers. Surely, it would be said, it is not the role of a planning system to tell people what they should do with their own house or to intervene in disputes between neighbours. However, many householders would argue that they expect the planning system to resolve disputes between neighbours. For example, questions of overlooking and loss of light are matters that should be resolved and can be handled by fairly straightforward regulations. It must be said, though, that many disputes between householders concern complaints that a proposal is unsightly or intrusive which are much more subjective concepts and need to be resolved by independent professional judgment. In Britain, planning applications from private householders make up a very significant proportion of total applications[9] and there have been suggestions from time to time that control should be relaxed for this type of applicant, thus achieving a reduction in the workload of planning departments and giving more freedom to owners and their architects. Whether or not this is achievable would depend on the position taken on the purpose of design control in existing residential areas. There are at least three options:

1. insistence on a high uniform quality of good design in order to maintain and enhance the appearance of the building stock, irrespective of individual and short-term wishes;
2. resolution of conflicts between neighbours irrespective of wider considerations;
3. achievement of design objectives required by the characteristics of the particular neighbourhood.

Clearly (1) is incompatible with relaxation of control on householder applications while (2) would preclude their total abolition. Purpose (3) would lead explicitly to spatial variation in the intensity of control. If any relaxation is to be achieved, then (3) combined with achievement of a 'bottom-line' version of (2) through regulations is the likely outcome.

Whatever position is taken on these controversies, calls for spatial variation in the intensity of control are

a matter to be reckoned with and are unlikely to disappear. Anyone drawing up a system for design control would be well advised, therefore, to make it capable of accommodating such variation should political circumstances so require it.

Summary

To recap, the essential points that have been identified in this chapter are:

- action to control the design of town and country is a political necessity;
- it must embrace urban design in its widest sense;
- it takes place in a pluralist context where the planning authority is but one actor among others;
- a control system must be seen as:
  - essential and positive;
  - rooted in value statements;
  - able to deal with many, often conflicting, values;
  - able to cope with variations in the degree of intervention.

Notes and references

1. L. Keeble (1971) *Town Planning at the Crossroads*, London: Estates Gazette, p. 171.
2. Notably J. V. Punter (1985) *A History of Aesthetic Control I: The Control of the External Appearance of Development in England and Wales, 1909–1947*, University of Reading, Working papers in Land Management and Development, Environmental Policy No. 2; Punter (1985) *A History of Aesthetic Control II: The Control of the External Appearance of Development in England and Wales, 1947–1985*, University of Reading, Working papers in Land Management and Development, Environmental Policy No. 7; also available as: Punter (1985) A history of aesthetic control, part 1 1909–1953. *Town Planning Review*, 57(4), 351–81; and Punter (1987) A history of aesthetic control, part 2 1953–1985. *Town Planning Review*, 58(1), 29–62.
3. See for example the arguments of Michael Manser which can be found in M. Manser (1991) Barriers to design. *RIBA Journal*, 86, 401–3; M. Manser and R. Adam (1992) Restoration of democracy mooted as architects

remodel system. *Planning*, 983, 16–17; and M. Manser and R. Adam (1992) Putting planning in better shape. *Planning*, 984, 24–5.

4. W. R. Ashby (1956) *An Introduction to Cybernetics*, London: Chapman & Hall, ch. 11.

5. At least in British practice. The final position reached can be gauged from: Dept. of Environment (1992), *Development Plans: A Good Practice Guide*, London: HMSO, Ch. 3.

6. Dept. of Environment (1980) *Circular 22/80: Development Control Policy and Practice*. London: HMSO, paras 19–20. The guidance was repeated in DoE (1988) *Circular 31/85: Aesthetic Control* and *Planning Policy Guidance Note 1*, paras 27–9.

7. House of Commons (1985) Command 9571, *Lifting the Burden*, London: HMSO.

8. See P. Hall (1988) *Cities of Tomorrow*, Oxford: Basil Blackwell, pp. 260 and 355; and R. Banham, P. Barker, P. Hall and C. Price (1969) Non–plan: an experiment in freedom. *New Society*, 26, 435–43.

9. Audit Commission for Local Authorities and the NHS for England and Wales (1992) *Building for Quality – A Study of Development Control, Local Government Report No. 7*, London: HMSO, p. 11.

Chapter 2

LIMITATIONS OF THE EXISTING SYSTEM – THE BRITISH EXPERIENCE

The limitations of a control system with regard to statements of design policy can best be appreciated by considering an example, in this case the British situation.[1] Given the argument of Chapter 1 that design control is politically inevitable but could, nevertheless, be pursued in a more sophisticated and flexible manner, it is necessary to highlight the impediments that prevent the British system achieving the objectives the public may require of it. The discussion will look firstly at features of the overall operation of the system of design control and then at the limitations of the existing formats.

Evolution of the British position

The changing ideas on the nature of control referred to in Chapter 1, and their manifestation in legal and administrative procedures, can be illustrated by British experience since 1947. The system introduced by the 1947 **Town and Country Planning Act** took for granted that a unique plan present in map form could be prepared to represent the public interest in each urban area. Design control was not explicitly mentioned but there is evidence that it was intended. What was not current at the time was the public consideration of alternative policies and the active involvement of interest groups and the public at large in the process. The public interest was seen as singular, divinable by the public authority and expressed in the development plan. The control function was intended as a necessary way of ensuring that new development was in accordance with the plan. However, during the 1960s the rate of change in economic and social conditions outstripped the ability of a develop-ment plan in the form of a land-use map to cope. Development plans took far longer to prepare and approve than had been envisaged. A timetable of quinquennial reviews made little progress and the original town and county maps became outdated. Nevertheless planning consent was still required by law and decisions on planning applications had still to be made. Development control continued almost as an end in itself, perpetuating what had become its own intrinsic values. In other words, a professional culture filled the gap in policy. This culture is still with us.

The 1970s saw the introduction of a new develop-ment plan system incorporating legal, administrative and plan-making procedures that were indicative of a new planning philosophy. The development plan had begun to be seen as a broad-based strategy emerging from a choice between value-based alternatives. Whereas this thinking had a great effect on plan making at the structure plan level it did not, unfortu-nately, percolate down to a more detailed level. Local plans did, indeed, become more methodical and directed towards control activities (especially during the 1980s) but this was not sufficient to counteract what had become a development control culture. What had much more effect on the conduct of design control was that the participation of interest groups and the public at large became fashionable. The planner was no longer seen as the sole arbiter of the public interest in the development process but as one agency in a plural-ist context. It is not argued here that all these ideas were quickly and effectively realized in practice (quite the contrary). What is significant is that they were embodied in legal and administrative changes that still characterize the British system. Noteworthy were the use of briefs for development setting out the position of the planning authority as a basis for negotiation on a particular site and Section 106 Agreements[2] by which developers may agree with the planning authority to use proceeds of the development for community benefit.

Degree of intervention

The notable point about British practice is that whereas detailed design control, especially the regulation of the external appearance of non-historic buildings, is not provided for explicitly in the legislation (or many statutory development plans) it is, nevertheless, a major feature of the day-to-day operation of town and country planning in Britain and is pursued with vigour by development control officers. Some may ask what the evidence for vigour is. It is true that detailed studies of day-to-day decision-making by development control officers are rather few, presumably because of the expense of carrying out such studies. A notable example was the study of the use of planning conditions by Beer and Booth[3] in the 1970s where 63 per cent of conditions were found to relate to functional aspects of design. Studies by the author[4] of the application of computer visualization to design control have also encountered a high degree of control over the detailed design of residential extensions exercised by local planning officers. In 1993, the point was well illustrated by an exhibition[5] staged at the RIBA of the effects planning intervention in particular cases. Moreover, it was difficult to find suitable cases of development in existing residential areas showing a high degree of freedom and personal choice when seeking examples to illustrate Chapter 3. In most areas there was none at all, and examples referred to by the local planning officers represented very marginal departures from the status quo. Such detailed intervention persists in spite of attempts by the central government since 1980 to limit the degree of control exercised in practice by local planning authorities.

Lack of explicit policy

When compared to procedures in other parts of the developed world, the most intriguing feature of the British system is the high degree of discretion given to the actors in the process at all levels. Development plans, though legal documents, are not legally binding on planning authorities when considering applications for planning permission. Appeals against refusal of planning permission may be made to the central government but, in practice, there are few constraints placed on the discretion of the appropriate minister and civil servants. This degree of discretion has both advantages and disadvantages. The benefit derives from the fact that the system is, in consequence, very flexible and can respond rapidly to exceptional or changing circumstances. In addition, the distortions in design produced by the over-rigid application of rules and specifications can be avoided as particular circumstances and the spirit and intention of the regulations can readily be taken into account. The problems arise from the lack of certainty for the public in general and potential applicants in particular. The policy of the planning authority can often be determined only by placing an application for permission in order to test the situation. The uncertainty is compounded by the fact that, not only are statutory development plans not legally binding, but there is an overall shortage of such plans. There is, indeed, complete coverage of Great Britain by structure plans (regional reports in Scotland and unitary development plans in the major conurbations) but at the lower tier, where local plans set out the more detailed land-use allocations, the situation is far from complete. Although the central government now requires total coverage, at the time of writing the process of providing it was still under way.

The interesting point is that a very comprehensive system of development control could exist and function in the absence of a statutory plan for it to implement. It should be noted that for much of the land area covered by a typical structure plan no preferred land-use is indicated. The local plans, where they exist, cover some of the important functional aspects of urban design (mix of uses, access, movement of pedestrians and vehicles) but do not deal with aesthetic or detailed matters except in terms of general policy (see discussion below). There may be other non-statutory documents dealing with urban design and landscape issues (such as design guides and other documents which are dealt with below) but there is even less national coverage by this less formal guidance than there is for local plans. Where there is more detailed specification of policy, in local plans or by other means, it is more likely to be for a town centre or area of particular historic or aesthetic value. The enhancement of the design of outlying residential and industrial areas (especially the latter) is hardly ever touched upon. It might be assumed that in the absence of a published policy a *laissez-faire* or non-plan policy applied. If this was the case it would be helpful to an applicant for it to be publicly known in advance. In the event, there is no evidence from any sources for the existence of anything approaching a non-plan policy, with the possible exception of Enterprise and Simplified Planning Zones. Moreover, when seeking examples for this book of cases of residential extensions that showed a high degree of personal expression, it was almost impossible to find ones that differed greatly from those conventionally acceptable to the planning profession and the impression of uniformly close scrutiny was obtained.

The absence of design policy available in advance of applications being made creates a number of problems. Firstly, potential applicants are in the dark about whether permission would be likely to be granted and whether preparatory work on the proposal would be worth while. This results in more time than need be being spent on pre-application consultations, abortive applications and appeals at a considerable cost to both applicants, their agents, and to the planning officers. The second problem is of concern to the public in general and the neighbours to a proposed development in particular. When an application for planning permission is made, the local planning authority responds and it is only then that its policy becomes apparent. Objectors to the proposal have to organize themselves after the application has been made. If what they are objecting to is also the latent policy of the planning authority then they are in a weak position (as they cannot appeal against the granting of a permission) and their only recourse is to lobby their councillors. If this lobbying is successful, and the permission is refused, much time and money will still have been lost both to application and objectors. In all these cases, the interests of all the participants would be served if prospective design policies were published in advance, objections received and the policy then publicly adopted and published (as is the case for the Structure and Local plans). There would then be fewer abortive applications, appeals and objections and much time would be saved across the board.

The discussion so far could be taken to imply that each local planning authority possessed a united view

within itself on urban design policy, especially the aesthetic aspects, but that, being unpublished it was hidden from view. However, this is not necessarily so and it is a plausible assumption that, in many cases, the authority is, like the neighbours to a proposed development, merely reacting to a proposal after the event with the officers having to think on their feet. For example, do those authorities (the majority?) that publish no guidance on the design of house extensions possess an internal document? If they do, why do they not reveal it? If they do not, how do they maintain consistency of judgment between their officers? The design of residential extensions does not figure prominently as a topic in the curriculum of most planning courses. How then are planning officers inducted into the knowledge they use when making recommendations on such applications? The impression is one of an informal planning culture passed on by word of mouth to new entrants to the profession.

There is another problem resulting from the lack of overall urban design policies that places significant, although often unacknowledged, limitations on the realizing of urban design objectives. The British system proceeds on an application by application basis. The planning authority cannot normally give legal permissions in advance of an application being made and, although it could use its good offices to promote development, it cannot guarantee that development will take place. In the absence of an overall urban design framework to inform the judgment on each application, and without positive incentives for developers to submit applications and provide urban infrastructure, achieving a co-ordinated approach to public spaces, for example, may often be a matter of chance rather than design.

Unfortunately, the shortage of plans and other policy guidance is not the only problem. There are also the difficulties caused by the limited scope of those documents that are produced. These are now dealt with in turn below.

Local plans

As remarked above, British structure and local plans had not been seen in the past as appropriate vehicles for urban design policies and, for most planning authorities, there were neither published design policies nor frameworks that could contain them. Fortunately, such evidence that had now become available had indicated a significant trend towards greater design content in British development plans in recent years. Studies of the design content of the unitary development plans in London by Gould[6] and structure and local plans in England and Wales by Punter for the Department of the Environment[7] were undertaken during 1992 and 1993 respectively. As a result of decisions by the central government, almost all local plans in England and Wales had to be prepared anew at this time, and many planning authorities had appeared to take advantage of this process to introduce greater design content.

The local plan is concerned with general land-use allocation, including significant areas of open space, and the identification of the principal road network and other major transport facilities. The plan usually contains clearly specified policies which are listed, numbered and designed to be used directly in the development control process. The introduction of this type of policy specification during the 1980s was a great improvement in the professionalization of the planning process. However, as far as urban design is concerned, these policies have limited value. Local plans usually contain policies which are in the nature of general aims or goals, often referred to as **motherhood statements**, for example, 'a high standard of design will be sought'. Statements of this nature are difficult to argue with. Would we expect a high standard not to be sought? The sentiment is laudable but does not take the reader very far. The frequent use of such words as 'suitable' and 'appropriate' can beg the question as, for example, in 'to provide suitable parking facilities in the town centre'. Suitable for whom? How is the reader to know what is suitable? This is often also a confusion of means and ends. Providing parking facilities is not an end in itself but a means of achieving objectives and these objectives should be stated. Analysis of problems and identification of issues may be provided but rarely is the linking argument through to prescription provided. However, this does not go far enough to meet the criticisms advanced here.

Outside conservation areas, Enterprise Zones and Simplified Planning Zones, local plans rarely contain design policies that apply to particular parts of the plan area only. A common construction is 'when A occurs then B will apply'. For example, 'In residential schemes, when because of the form of development, it

is appropriate to provide communal car parking this should be provided close to the dwellings it serves and designed to encourage maximum use'.[8] This may seem innocuous as far as it goes but it does not say where schemes would be appropriate. It does not arise from local circumstances. Statements of this type do not view local neighbourhoods as a whole and such rules of thumb could result in an action that is inappropriate for a particular area. Whereas there may be a need for this type of statement in some instances, it cannot be a substitute for policies that relate to the requirements of subdivisions of the local plan area.

Local plans also create a more subtle problem for urban design through their land-use allocations. Allocating preferred land-uses such as **residential** or **commercial** to a parcel of land may not be the most important issue as far as the design of many urban areas is concerned and could even obstruct the realization of other design objectives. Take, for example, the Georgian square. This form in the original concept comprised town houses around a communal garden. The contemporary design objectives may be to maintain the structure and decoration of the buildings, the planting and public use of the garden, efficient public access and to limit pollution from traffic. These could be (and are) achieved with the buildings in residential, commercial or educational use, sometimes all three within the same square. Moreover, most contemporary urban designers would argue that a mix of uses was desirable in itself and should be a major design objective. Unfortunately, the standard form of the local plan does not lend itself to such a prescription. (It is true that some local plans allocate **town centre uses** in appropriate locations but this does not remove the general objection.)

It is not the primary intention of the local plan to provide detailed design guidance and the criticisms to be presented here must not, therefore, be seen as criticism of local plans as such. It is rather that their limitations must be recognized as they are the only part of the statutory development plan that impinges directly on urban design.

Standards

Many (most?) local planning authorities publish design standards within their local plans, design guides and

11

informal policy statements. The standards for special topics are sometimes available as separate documents. The characteristics of standards are numerical specification of the required quantities or dimensions which apply either universally or in an 'if A exists then B will apply' form. Examples are minimum size of private gardens, back-to-back distances between houses, minimum numbers of garages and/or parking spaces and width of carriageways and footpaths. Their general use in planning was reviewed in the 1970s by Woodford[9] but there has, unfortunately, been no recent equivalent. The problem with standards as an expression of design policy is that, because of their inflexibility, they are not tailored to the process of negotiation. They relate to the outputs of the design process rather than its inputs. Therefore, rather than the parties to negotiation being able to agree a common intention and then proceed to an agreed design concept, they find that, whatever their intentions, certain aspects of the design are predetermined. *In extremis*, a design for a housing layout could be almost pre-determined by a multiplicity of standards. Moreover, it is not always made clear how the standards have been derived from broader policies. For example, planning authorities have produced in the past leaflets on parking standards applying to areas for which no local plan had been prepared. The best argument for the use of standards is that they are useful for holding the line and preventing the use of 'salami tactics' by developers. Whereas this may be an essential part of the operation of development control, it cannot be said that standards are a creative instrument of design guidance, nor a substitute for proper design policy.

Conditions

The conditions attached to planning permissions are not really **policy** as discussed above but, where statements of design policy are absent, they form the means of deducing the latent policy by implication from the control decisions. The extensive study by Beer and Booth[10] showed that, at least around 1980, they were certainly used to control design aspects of proposed development. However, they are no substitute for proper design policies and share all the limitations of standards and density specifications. Although, unlike

them, they can be the result of negotiation, they are still the outputs rather than the inputs of the design process. Although some planning authorities do publish lists of their standard conditions, their derivation from policy may not be explicit. In the past, as with standards, there may have been no local plan from which they could be derived. Moreover, many standard conditions contrive to further conceal the latent policy. For example, a very common design condition is 'landscaping shall be to the satisfaction of the planning authority'. There is usually no way of the applicant knowing in advance what will satisfy the authority other than informal conversations with individual officers. The applicant ultimately has to submit an application to test the condition. The problem, as with the absence of design policy in general, is the uncertainty and difficulty in ensuring consistency.

Conservation areas

Since their introduction in 1967, conservation areas have proved to be very popular devices with over 8000 now designated and almost all British local planning authorities possessing them. They are comparatively easy to designate, this being almost exclusively a matter for the local authority concerned and with no binding criteria laid down in the legislation or by central government. Their principal legal power is the control of demolition, something that has not always been available automatically in British town planning legislation.[11] There is also an assumption made that they are to be used for notably historic areas and should be accompanied by a positive programme of enhancement. However, practice on this point can be extremely variable ranging from expensive and well-researched restoration schemes to merely the drawing of a line on a map. Whereas the lack of information in many conservation areas has been a long-standing problem, there has been a growing and welcome trend in the best authorities towards explanatory leaflets and, in some cases, substantial illustrated guides. An important source of information on this point has been the study of conservation area practice commissioned by the RTPI from Chestertons and Central England University.[12] It revealed a notable tendency during the mid 1970s and early 1980s to establish general policies for conservation, especially in the south-east of the country. More significantly, there was a movement towards the production of guides for individual areas which peaked in mid 1970s and again in the late 1980s. Both trends now appear to be continuing through the 1990s. Nevertheless, although many planning authorities may now provide detailed analysis and guidance, often of an exemplary nature, for too many British conservation areas the only documentation has been a line on a map, an issue that has resulted in correspondence in professional journals.[13]

Good as they may be, explanatory guides to historic context are not the same as design policy. Conservation means that some elements of urban form are to be presented while others may be subject to modification or even removal. The distinction between them should be deduced from the objective(s) causing the original designation of the conservation area. What exactly are the characteristics that must be retained? Some conservation area guides imply the existence of particular objectives although these are rarely made explicit. In some famous historic areas (such as the centre of Bath) the issue is fairly obvious and preservation should be the dominant concern. However, as more imaginative use is made of the concept by applying it to areas without obvious dramatic historic features, so the need to be more specific regarding the intention behind the designation becomes more necessary.[14]

Design guides

For the twenty years or more before the early 1990s, and to a large extent after, the principal source for anything approximating to urban design policies lay in the supplementary guidance that was published by planning authorities but which was not part of the statutory development plan. These are often collectively referred to as 'design guides' . From the Essex design guide[15] onwards, they have become a distinctive feature of British planning and their production has become more frequent and more diverse with the passage of time. It is difficult to see them other than being a very positive step towards more effective design control. They have unfortunately, though, been limited in their scope.

Their occurrence and content has been reviewed on three occasions:

- in 1976 by the Department of the Environment;[16]
- in 1985 as part of the *Time for Design* initiative;[17]
- in 1992 by Birmingham Polytechnic.[18]

The material collected for the 1992 Birmingham study has also been examined independently by the author. The 1976 study revealed little use of design guides but by the time of the 1985 investigation a considerable number was in use. Their coverage, though, was far from universal and represented probably only a minority of authorities. Taking 'no response' as indicating 'no guide' the proportion using guides was still under half in 1992. From a review of these investigations the following points relevant to the argument emerged:

- The most common form of guide was a leaflet, usually dealing with the appearance of residential extensions or shop fronts, and applying to all parts of the authority's area.
- Explicit mention and articulation of goals and objectives were rare.
- There was little feel for wider urban design principles embracing the inter-relationship of buildings, spaces and movement.
- There was almost nothing on industrial areas[19] in spite of increasingly controversial design problems resulting from conversion to retail and leisure uses.
- A few county councils produced comprehensive highways guides, some with only a 'standards' approach but others[20] showing much sophistication and a forward looking perspective. Unfortunately, they were rarely linked to overall urban design policies, particularly those applied to three-dimensions.
- There was no comprehensive design guide (with the possible and recent exception of Suffolk[21]) that approached the coverage of the Essex guide.

The last point was particularly disappointing in the light of the age of this guide and its need of revision. This revision was belatedly taking place[22] but the delay should have encouraged other planning authorities to fill the gap.

A difficulty for all guides has been that often more has been read into them than their authors intended. The normal intention was that they should provide guidance, that is ways of achieving good design, without placing arbitrary or unnecessary restriction on developers and their professional advisors. However, some planning authorities have not only adopted them as policy but applied their content as standards. Some developers have taken the suggestions too literally. For example, the Essex guide attempted to encourage the use of the local vernacular for aesthetic inspiration. Its illustrations of Essex styles have become a style in themselves which has been transferred to inappropriate locations such as the London Docklands. Even if the guides are properly used and interpreted, it is unfair to see them as providing a solution to the problem of lack of design policy and to judge them accordingly.

Their most important limitation is, as remarked above, that they do not cover all types of development, industrial estates being a notable omission. Whereas guidance on new residential areas, shop fronts and house extensions are strong themes, they make no attempt to deal with the requirements of particular neighbourhoods. They rarely relate their suggestions to specific goals, especially those stemming from wider planning policies. Moreover, they are not available, by a long way, in all parts of the country.

Design briefs

Design briefs state the requirements of the planning authority for a particular site and are a vital part of the process of design control. Unfortunately, little was published on them between the late 1970s and the early 1990s.[23] As remarked in Chapter 1, their emergence was a clear admission that the control process consisted of negotiation between several parties. The RTPI[24] has seen the design brief as a special case of the planning brief, its intention being to set out the position of the planning authority towards a site for which development is imminent. It should make clear those elements of a possible design that the planning authority would regard as being essential, those that could be open to negotiation or are made as suggestions, and those that are, by implication, left to the discretion of the developer. In practice, the quality of briefs can vary widely and they are not used by all planning authorities in all circumstances. However, even if high-quality briefs were universally used, the fact that they are site- and time-specific means that they can never be a substitute for statements of wider urban design policy. On the contrary, they should stem from such plans. It is inter-

esting to speculate where, in the absence of design policies for particular areas, the design briefs have their origin. Presumably, we are back to the personal judgment and discretion of the planning officers.

Density controls

The specification of density is often resorted to as a means of controlling the design of a residential area (whether expressed in terms of dwellings, habitable rooms, bed-spaces or persons per unit area). It has the advantage of being a measure that is easily calculated and communicated. Town maps prepared under the 1947 Town and Country Planning Act contained cartograms that specified the density for each allocation of residential land-use. Unfortunately, in the absence of strong central government backing, they proved difficult to sustain on appeal and did not survive the subsequent changes to the development plan system. They have, nevertheless, survived in a much more informal role. The problem from the urban design perspective is that, whereas density specifications place limits on the type of urban form that can be built, they do not determine it. They can be said to put the cart before the horse in that the density ought to result from decisions about the design rather than presage it. Density is not a tangible concept such as vehicle access and open space. Neither does it say anything about who can use spaces created by, say, reducing the density. This point is well argued by Bishop and Davison[25] who draw the distinction between the use of density controls as either a 'shield' or as a 'sword'. This is equivalent to the conclusion arrived at above on the use of **standards** and **conditions** in design control. These may be needed sometimes as a procedural defence, or shield, but they are no substitute for positive objectives, or sword.

International comparisons

These comments on British planning practice can be thrown into relief by reference to the position overseas. The comparative study of planning systems in developed countries, with particular emphasis on detailed planning and control procedures, has been gaining ground for some years to the immediate enrichment of academic study and, hopefully, to the benefit of planning practice in the longer term. An introductory account of the planning systems of Denmark, France, Germany, the Netherlands and Great Britain is provided by the study commissioned by the Department of the Environment from Reading University[26] and accounts of the development control systems in the United States are provided by Delafons[27] and Wakeford.[28] At one level, these studies reveal a wide variation in practice from highly complex regulations to a wide degree of discretion. As far as design (or, frequently, just aesthetic) control goes, there is a range from detailed prescription to a near absence of policy. Within the United States this variation exists within the country itself. However, within this diversity there are certain general patterns and, possibly, lessons to be learnt. Wakeford holds the view that Britain and the United States could be on a convergent course and Delafons[29] has suggested that the British system could benefit from some of the aspects of American practice. As mentioned previously, the British system is marked by the great degree of discretion accorded to the responsible authorities and, at first sight it would appear that the principle of **legislation binding all parties** and **policies for small areas**, as found in many American states and some Western European countries, could go a long way to meeting some of the deficiencies chronicled here.

However, whereas there would undoubtedly be benefit in the British system moving more in this direction, it does not follow that the practice in other countries already embodies all the answers to problems of design control. With regard to policies for small areas, the Dutch Bestimmingsplan provides a good example of detailed land-use specification. Unfortunately, they are not normally a vehicle for three-dimensional characteristics, explicitly aesthetic policy or similar urban design considerations. There is also the problem of revision, the difficulty in keeping such a detailed plan up-to-date. Danish plans can contain three-dimensional proposals but this is not a common practice and has overtones of a master-plan approach rather than that of an aid to negotiation. It is, of course, difficult to review the operation of the systems, particularly any recent innovations, in the countries mentioned within the confines of these paragraphs. Nevertheless, the point must be made that

major initiatives in the specification of urban design policy on the lines proposed in Chapter 3 have not yet come to light.

Given the previously critical reception on both sides of the Atlantic of what was seen as a weak tradition of planning practice, the attention shown to American operations has been remarkable. The praise directed at the settlement of Seaside, Florida, by the Prince of Wales[30] and his advisers has been particularly notable. Delafons and others have drawn attention to the untypicality of Seaside but, nevertheless believe that there is much to learn from the general practice of policies for **zones** and the complex and binding regulations by which they are implemented. The point is well made that, for many parts of the United States, development is regulated to a degree unknown in Britain and with no right of appeal. Zoning, whereby land-use regulations are specified for small areas is, perhaps, the best known feature of the American system and it does provide a vehicle that focuses attention on the position of neighbourhoods and other small areas.

However, American planners and academic critics find it surprising that their system should attract any admiration from British commentators when the quality of the environment of American cities is self-evidently and dramatically inferior to that appertaining in their European equivalents. Even allowing for cultural differences, there must be something in the European systems, especially the British one, that produces their higher quality physical environment. The problem for the United States system would appear to lie in its lack of specification of urban design policy rather than its development control procedures, varying as they do from the negligible to the draconian. Habe[31] has reviewed the design content of plans in the United States and has found that, although there are many of them, they tend to concerned with surface appearance and aesthetics rather than more comprehensive urban design goals.[32] Seaside may be superficially attractive to the eye but it is a second-home quasi-recreational facility without meaning for the general problems of inner city and suburb. Contrasting the disorder of the American scene with the almost artificial neatness of Dutch residential development it is difficult to see the output from the different systems other than as a product of their adaptation to their political and cultural context. Control systems, in particular the specification of design policy, must encompass this fact.

Reasons for the lack of policy

This chapter has argued that what is lacking is:

- policy with an urban design content, e.g. functional relationship of spaces, aesthetic issues;
- clear statements of goals and objectives that can discussed at the appropriate times and places;
- policy that reflects the particular requirements of small areas;
- policy for all land-use types including industrial areas, and the less interesting parts of town, even if it is of a non-plan nature.

If the omissions can be so clearly stated, it is legitimate to ask why they have not been remedied. One response that the author has encountered is that there is an almost infinite number of possible variations possible in the appearance of proposed development which no policy statement could possibly anticipate. The reply to this argument must be that a planning system exists in order to deal with uncertainty, and strategies and tactics to cope with a variety of outcomes should be its basic characteristics. Indeed, such evidence of design control practice as exists indicates that underlying principles are often applied by planning offices even if they are not fully articulated and published. For example, rooflines, building lines and prevention of overshadowing are all in evidence in actual decisions. What is needed is for them to be written down. Another objection is often that publication of design policy is unnecessary as 'they can always ask'. This response presupposes that a great deal of staff time will be available to deal with enquiries, a somewhat unlikely assumption. Even in the event of such a resource being available, it would be an inefficient way of deploying staff and there is always the crucial problem of ensuring consistency between officers. (It is not being suggested here that professional officers should not deal with queries from the public but that this can be no substitute for published information.) A further objection is that to publish any detailed design policy would precipitate political controversy and alarm local amenity groups. Again, the response must be that this dealing with differences is what the planning system is there for. It must surely be more efficient to settle a controversy in advance of detailed work being undertaken than to have it arise after an application for planning permission has been submitted.

It is interesting, without digressing too much, to examine the relevance to the arguments of this book of the criticisms of the British planning system made by Reade.[33] When first published they aroused much controversy and were rejected by many (if not most) practitioners. He was concerned by the lack of interest shown by planners in the success or failure of planning practice when judged against its overall goals or, indeed, in the political significance, or even very existence, of these goals. His accounts[34] of his actual experience of local authority actions (or, rather, the lack of them) while living in a conservation area in Bangor, North Wales, provide a direct and vivid expression of his criticism. He conveys the impression of local engineers and planning officers[35] being more concerned with the operation of their procedures than with what they were supposed to be achieving. He has subsequently re-stated his point[36] that many planning policies, conservation areas being a particular example, serve to maintain and increase property values for particular groups in society and are therefore overtly political in nature and should be handled as such. There is a certain correspondence between some of his arguments and the general message of this book, i.e.:

- British planning has a structure which presupposes political accountability;
- there is an informal office culture incorporating a reliance on procedures and individual judgment that creates the appearance of a non-political process;
- there is the fear that the goals, explicit or hidden, are not in fact being achieved and that operation of the process becomes a substitute for their fulfilment.

The most likely reason why there is a lack of published design policy, not only in Britain but most parts of Western Europe and North America, is that such plans are not compulsory and, in a hard-pressed office, it is the legally required development plans and control procedures that take precedence. However, even if design plans were legally required, genuine obstacles to progress would still be encountered. There are reasons, other than pressure of work, why there is a reluctance to issue such documents.

One important issue is that of means of communication of design policies to others. The problem is how to put over the distinction between what is essential and what can be allowed to vary. A photograph or drawing of, say, a building in its context is a direct way of communicating an intention. However, the picture presented will contain not only the representation of the essential point but also much detail that is not part of it. How can the viewer avoid picking up the detail rather than the point intended? How can bias be avoided? Words can and are used to indicate the essentials of policies but they lack the power and immediacy of pictures. This difficulty is clearly an obstacle to the preparation of design policy. It is pursued further in Chapter 6 where it is suggested that information technology can provide a solution.

However, the most significant obstacle is the lack of a methodology that addresses all the limitations identified above and is available in a convenient form. The area of strategic planning has benefited from the assimilation of demographic, economic and other research methods which has led to an identifiable body of theory and practice that can be used in plan-making. Although there is theoretical work that could have been drawn upon, no such corpus exists for the preparation of design plans. There has been an understandable concentration on actual outcomes ('good design') and on who makes the decisions but little attention has been given to the process of preparing policy. It is not easy to develop such policy without a handbook, particularly when working under pressure. Concepts such as **character**, **fitting in** and **high standard of design** can be employed as a cipher for very complex issues and it is understandable that planning officers needing to make quick decisions will not be able to rush out complicated documents without some form of methodology expressed in a convenient form.

Summary

To summarize, we could say that the British planning system is marked by a high degree of officer discretion and a lack of policy documentation relating to urban design, particularly for small areas. Local plans, design guides, and design briefs are produced which, within their own objectives can be professional and effective instruments. However, not only do they not cover the whole country, but they do not attempt to address all aspects of design policy, nor do they relate explicitly to wider planning policy. The resulting lack of

published policy causes expense and inconvenience to the public at large and to all parties to the development process, not least the planning officers themselves.

What is needed are statements of policy that:

- cover all aspects of urban design;
- specify intentions towards small areas;
- cover all areas including those of little visual interest and those where an open and flexible policy applies;
- are useful for negotiation in the development and planning processes, especially the political aspects.

To achieve them there is a need to develop a methodology that will assist planning professionals in the preparation of such policy statements. Theoretical and practical work exists on urban design principles, townscape studies and urban morphology that can contribute to such a methodology. Computer-based methods can greatly aid the communication of such policies and make them accessible to a lay audience. The first step must be the development of clear and more systematic thinking on the problem. The following chapter attempts to set out how this could be done.

Notes and references

1. For those unfamiliar with the overall structure of the British planning there are useful summaries in: the DoE/Reading University survey of planning in Western Europe: Dept. of Environment (1989) *Planning Control in Western Europe*, London: HMSO, pp. 33–78; and in the report on planning in Britain undertaken by the Nuffield Foundation: Nuffield Foundation (1986) *Town and Country Planning: A report of the committee of inquiry appointed by the Nuffield Foundation*, London: Nuffield Foundation, Chs 1 and 2; and in J. Hillman (1990) *Planning for Beauty*, London: Royal Fine Art Commission, HMSO. The development of the approach to design control adopted in Britain has been conveniently set out in P. Booth (1987) Design control. In M. L. Harrison and R. Mordey (eds), *Planning Control: Philosophies Policy and Practice*, London, Sydney and Wolfeboro NH: Croom Helm; and Punter, note 2, Chapter 1.
2. Section 106 of the Town and Country Planning Act, 1990.

3. A. Beer and P. Booth (1981) *Development Control and Design Quality*, Sheffield: Sheffield Centre for Environmental Research. See also P. Booth (1983) Development control and design quality: Part 1 Conditions a useful way of controlling design? *Town Planning Review*, **54**(3), 265–84; and A. Beer (1983) Development control and design quality: Part 2 Attitudes to design. *Town Planning Review*, **54**(4), 383–404.

4. A. C. Hall (1993) The use of computer visualisation in planning control: an investigation of its utility in selected examples, *Town Planning Review*, **64**(2), 193–212.

5. R. Hawkins and P. Vigars (1993) *Before and After Planning*, Exhibition Guide, explained by the authors as R. Hawkins (1993) The planning process: what goes on behind closed doors. *The Architects' Journal*, 24 January, 16–17; and P. Vigars (1993) Before and after shot. *Planning*, 1002, 6–7. In Hall's opinion, most of the interventions illustrated were both necessary and beneficial. The exhibition was not of a negative character.

6. S. J. Gould (1992) *Design Policy in London's Unitary Development Plans*. Unpublished MPhil thesis, Dept. of Land Management and Development, Reading University. The findings of this work are summarized in Gould (1992) London's unitary development plans: design policy and control. *Urban Design Quarterly*, 44, 11–16.

7. J. V. Punter, M. Carmona and P. Platts (1994) Design policies in development plans. *Urban Design Quarterly*, 51, 11–15.

8. Wycombe District Council (1994) *Wycombe District Local Plan*.

9. G. Woodford *et al.* (1976) *The Value of Standards in the External Residential Environment*, DoE Research Report No. 6. London: HMSO.

10. Beer and Booth, note 2.

11. Before the 1990 Town and Country Planning Act, the view was that only listed buildings and buildings in conservation areas were subject to demolition control as demolition was not development The Courts subsequently held that demolition was development. This was confirmed by the 1992 Planning and Compensation Act but the General Development Order was amended in 1993 to make demolition permitted development for all properties except for private dwelling houses. There is, therefore, no control over the demolition of non–residential buildings outside conservation areas.

12. Royal Town Planning Institute (1993) *The Character of Conservation Areas*. Commissioned Study from Chesterton Consulting and University of Central England, London: RTPI.

13. See, for example, the letter from David Morton (1991) in *Planning*, 924, 2; the editorial, A. Fyson (1991) The threat to ancient towns. *The Planner*, 77(21), 3; and the letter from Stewart Squires (1991) in *The Planner* 77(30), 6.

14. This message has been reinforced by Dept. of Environment (1994) *Historic Buildings and Conservation Areas*, PPG 15, London: HMSO; and English Heritage (1993) *Conservation Area Practice*, London: English Heritage.

15. Essex County Council (1973) *A Design Guide for Residential Areas*, Chelmsford: Essex CC.

16. Dept. of Environment (1976) *Design Guidance Survey*, London: DoE.

17. Dept. of Environment (1990) *Time for Design: Monitoring the Initiative*, London, HMSO.

18. D. Chapman and P. Larkham (1992) *Discovering the Art of Relationship: Urban Design, Aesthetic Control and Design Guidance*, Research Paper No. 9, Faculty of the Built Environment, Birmingham Polytechnic (now the University of Central England).

19. For an exception to this trend see Essex County Council (1984) *South Woodham Ferrers: Western Industrial Area Design Brief*.

20. A leading example was the Devon County Council (1992) *Traffic Calming Guide*, Exeter: Devon CC. The guides issued by Cheshire, Kent and Surrey County Councils were also very significant for urban design.

21. Suffolk County Council (1994) *Suffolk Design Guide for Residential Areas*, Ipswich: Suffolk CC.

22. A. Stones, (1992) Revising the Essex Design Guide. *Urban Design Quarterly*, 44, 17–19.

23. A. Mandani-Pour, M. Lally and G. Underwood (1993) *Design Briefs in Planning Practice*, Working Paper 26, Dept. of Town and Country Planning, University of Newcastle-upon-Tyne.

24. RTPI (1990) *Practice Advice Note No. 8*, London: RTPI.

25. J. Bishop and I. Davison (1989) *Development Densities: A Discussion Paper*. Amersham: NHBRC and The Housing Research Foundation.

26. Dept. of Environment, note 1.

27. J. Delafons (1990) *Aesthetic Control: A report on the methods used in the USA to control the design of buildings*. Monograph 41. University of California at Berkeley, Institute of Urban and Regional Development.

28. R. Wakeford (1990) *American Development Control*, London: HMSO.

29. J. Delafons (1991) Design control – the American experience. Report of Proceedings, Town and Country

Planning Summer School, 1991. In *The Planner*, 77(40), 23–6. For a similar argument see B. Cullingworth (1991) Aesthetics in US planning: from billboards to design control. *Town Planning Review*, 62(4), 399–413.

30. HRH the Prince of Wales (1989) *A Vision of Britain: A Personal View of Architecture*, London: Doubleday.

31. R. Habe (1989) Public design control in American communities: design guidelines/design review. *Town Planning Review*, 60(2), 195–219.

32. For further discussion of US design plans see M. Southworth (1989) Theory and practice of contemporary urban design: a review of design plans in the United States. *Town Planning Review*, 60(4), 369–420.

33. E. Reade (1987) *British Town and Country Planning*, Milton Keynes: Open University Press.

34. E. Reade (1991/92) The little world of Upper Bangor. *Town and Country Planning*, 1991, 60(11/12), 340–3, 1992 61(1), 25–7 and 61(2), 44–7.

35. Reference is made here to the activities of planners, and also engineers, in contrast to public and political goals. It is likely, though, that architects acting for members of the public would also see the process as non-political, a matter for absolute aesthetic judgment, although by architects not planning departments.

36. As reported in I. Burton (1992) Planners in mystery play. *Planning*, 993, 17.

Chapter 3

A METHODOLOGY FOR DESIGN PLANS

Principles for design plans

Chapter 2 has argued that statements of policy on design relating to specific areas are necessary. This chapter proposes **design plans** and a method for generating them. The content of the design plans would be additional to existing land-use plans and would conform to them. There is room for debate on whether detailed design policies should be part of a statutory land-use plan or in a supplementary document but, whatever line is taken, the proposals made here would be equally applicable. Design plans should be produced for the territory of all planning authorities. Their realization may be some way off but a start can be made now on establishing a method.

It follows from the discussion in the previous chapter that design plans must embrace the following basic principles:

- they should embody urban design concepts, i.e. they should deal with statements of the desirable form, use and inter-relationship of buildings and landscapes and the spaces they define;
- they should facilitate negotiations between all parties to the development process, especially the controlling authority and including the public at large;
- they should relate to the continuing incremental redevelopment of urban areas;

and that design plans should possess the following characteristics:

1. they should distinguish between matters essential to the position of the planning authority and those that are negotiable;

2. they should distinguish between means and ends;
3. they should be able to handle value statements in the same currency as used by local politicians and members of the public;
4. they should possess the flexibility to be able to handle changes in both values and development characteristics over time;
5. they should incorporate statements that are area specific;
6. they should refer to all parts of the plan area irrespective of the priority, timeliness and degree of intervention by the planning authority.

The four-way split

To meet these requirements it is proposed that the design plan should be **objective driven**. Objectives are useful in negotiation to distinguish between what a party is aiming to achieve and such matters as the means of achieving it, the degree to which it may be achieved and what achieving it may mean in practice. If the point of difference between the negotiating parties lies in their objectives then it is better to clear this up at the outset otherwise much time will be wasted. Stating an objective implies an attempt to distinguish the intention from the end product. Too often in design control it has been the examples quoted in guides which have been copied rather than the philosophy behind them. It has been argued that the Essex design guide,[1] produced just the misunderstandings complained of. Builders have often followed its outward style rather that the basic philosophy.

Table 3.1 Principles of urban design (as collated by John Punter)

	Kevin Lynch 1982	Jane Jacobs 1961	Bentley Alcock McGlynn 1964 Murrain Smith	Tibbalds 1988	HRH The Prince of Wales 1989	Holyoak 1985	Urban Design Group 1987	Wates 1988	Buchanan 1988
1	Vitality (include biological and ecological)	Appropriate activity before visual order	'Responsive' environments	Places before buildings	The place		Responsive forms	Urban environment in broadest sense	Place making public realm outdoor rooms
2	(See sense)		Visual appropriateness	Respect history	Harmony and context	(i) Retain the best (ii) Respect street line			Dialogue with context and history: re-contain street
3	(See fit)	Mixed use mixed age, mixed rent concentration	Variety	Encourage mixed uses		More than one use	Mixed uses		
4	(See vitality)		Human scale	Scale enclosure	In scale with context				
5	Access	The street Permeability (short blocks)	Permeability	Encourage pedestrian permeability			Public access		Public space and movement systems
6	Control	Social mix and consultation	Personalization	Social mix and consultation	Community	'Acceptable' personalization	Consultation	Individual responsibility, professional enablers, local action and control, integrating experience, optimizing resources, environment, education	
7	Sense (clarity with which it can be perceived)		Legibility	Legibility	Hierarchy	Visual accessibility reflect uses			(i) Respect conventions (ii) Articulate meanings (iii) Connect inside and out
8	Fit (adaptability)	Robust spaces	Robustness and adaptability						
9	(See efficiency)	Gradual not cataclysmic money		Small scale change					
10	Two meta criteria efficiency (relative cost), justice (social equity)	Activity richness Automobile attrition surveillance (safety)	Richness	Visual delight	Materials and decoration Signs and lights	'Visible' construction integral ornament	Stimulating Protection security comfort shelter		Natural, rich materials good weathering decoration

Developing the distinction between intentions and ends together with idea of an objective-driven plan gives rise to the following **four-way split** for the content of design plans:

1. statement of the objectives;
2. criteria for the achievement of the objectives (performance standards); advisory material giving guidance on how the objectives might be fulfilled;
3. advisory material giving guidance on how the objectives might be fulfilled without necessarily limiting the possible options;
4. procedures that will, or may, be necessary in the process of fulfilling the objectives.

It is proposed that this four-way distinction should be at the heart of any design plan.

Design goals

Objectives must come from somewhere and the discussion of design objectives is largely the discussion of their generation. Objectives are more precise formulations of more general goals. The objectives must be achieved for the goals to be fulfilled. They differ from the goals in that their achievement can be specified by measurable criteria. The goals have utility in as much as their content corresponds with value statements used in the political process.[2] Once politically useful goals have been agreed then objectives can be deduced from them. However, the generation of neither the design goals nor the design objectives is a simple and straightforward matter. Indeed, as suggested at the end of Chapter 2, this very difficulty may be a frequent reason for the lack of effective design policy.

A way of overcoming such difficulties is to disaggregate the tasks, making distinctions between different types of goal. To start the process we can distinguish between:

1. general principles that should, in the opinion of the planning authority, govern all design;
2. goals specific to the particular plan area.

Taking the general principles first, many authors over the past 40 years have attempted to describe them in their books or to summarize them as a list of 'ten commandments'. Nine of them have been conveniently summarized by Punter[3] and his comparative table is reproduced as Table 3.1. As Punter, and others, have pointed out, the development of such principles is beset with pitfalls. To start with, there is the matter of **scope**. Should they, at one extreme, be concerned only with aesthetic criteria for judging the outward appearance of buildings? Alternatively, should they extend to matters such as ecological protection, reduction of pollution and the control of motor vehicles? Secondly, there is the issue of **degree of detail**. Should they be confined to one-line statements of general applicability or should they be elaborated into detailed codes? The answer lies in making the principles relevant to:

- the experiences of the likely users;
- the development process.

It could be argued that it is not sufficient just to lay down a number of one-line statements (such as the 'Ten Commandments' of the Prince of Wales[4] or those of Tibbalds,[5] worthy as they are), but to refer to a book or collection of writings which develop a design philosophy at greater length. The pre-eminent example is *Responsive Environments.*[6] This is a genuine attempt to promulgate a way of designing that incorporates definite 'people centred' values. Its seven principles of permeability, legibility, variety, robustness, visual appropriateness, richness and personalization require explanation and understanding and this is provided both by the book and by further study.

Another source of design goals is the Essex guide. As well as many policies that have stood the test of time there are also problems due mainly to the age of the guide. Its 'Design Policies – Physical' section betrays the confusion of means and ends discussed in Chapter 2, in effect promulgating standards rather than objectives. However, its 'Design Policies – Visual' section contains genuine goals that could be simply stated and effectively included in a design plan. They are reproduced as Figure 3.1. The authors propose under 'building design principles' what are, in effect, six general design goals and advocate what was the guide's special contribution, the goals of 'regional character' and 'space and identity'.

Regional character brings us to the second type of goal, that which is specific to the plan area in question. There can be a hierarchy and a logical progression of

3.0   DESIGN POLICIES – VISUAL

Approved by the County Planning Committee
Minute 21 January, 1973

3.1   The Principles of Spatial Organisation

New housing areas shall create a visually satisfactory
environment, achieved by employing either the
principles of:—
  (i) buildings set within a dominant landscape of a
      character indigenous to Essex; or
  (ii) built forms set to satisfactorily enclose spaces
      of individual identity.

3.4   Design of Buildings within the Urban Framework

3.41 Regional Character

To perpetuate the unique building character of the
county and to re-establish local identity, development shall generally employ external materials which
are sympathetic in colour and texture to the vernacular range of Essex materials.

3.44 Building Design Principles

Individual buildings shall be well designed of themselves and have adequate regard for their setting by
  (i) the building being designed to form part of the
      larger composition of the area in which it is
      situated;
  (ii) the building using suitable external materials
      for the location in which it is situated;
  (iii) the volumes making up the block form of the
      building being proportioned and related to
      form a satisfactory composition;
  (iv) the external materials being used in a visually
      appropriate manner;
  (v) the fenestration being well proportioned and
      well related within the elevation and also being
      sympathetic to adjacent buildings;
  (vi) architectural detailing being used to reinforce
      the character required by the design and its
      location.

levels, starting with statements of the desired **image** for the plan area. For National Parks and significant historic towns this is likely to be a clear and uncontroversial but for most other places it can present difficulties. If it is not thought possible to define an overall image then this should be clearly stated. At the opposite pole from historic images there are futuristic ones. In Britain in the late 1960s, Newcastle upon Tyne proclaimed itself the 'Brasilia of the North' and Leeds the 'Motorway City of the Seventies'. Such slogans conveyed design goals that were pursued in practice. The unfortunate (from the standpoint of the 1990s) content of these goals should not be allowed to obscure the important point that they were both publicly proclaimed and had design implications (unlike, say, 'Liverpool: a Socialist City' and 'Newport: Home of the Mole Wrench'). Many other cities across the world followed the same futuristic goals as Newcastle without making it plain (or, perhaps, even being aware) of where they were going. If a goal is made public, even as a slogan, it can then, if need be, be challenged by the public. If it is not, it cannot. Image statements will be of a general political nature and be expected to apply to the whole of the plan area.

Nevertheless, many will have effect only in certain parts of the area. Most historic towns and cities, even very famous ones such as York and Chester, have a significant core, where Roman and medieval forms are to be seen, but this is surrounded by substantial areas of twentieth-century housing and industry of less distinction. Unless it is desired eventually to rebuild the more recent development in historic form, there cannot be a single image statement that is both useful for design control (as opposed, say, to tourism) purposes and applicable to the town as a whole. They may be of the 'if A exists then B will apply' form. This type of statement was criticized in Chapter 2 as a substitute for detailed policy but it has its place as a design goal. The image statement may also be used to generate other goals. Goals that could be deduced from the image statement on the basis of the existing physical form of the plan area using townscape analysis. For example, design goals could be stated for the following topics.

- Entrances to the urban area by road, rail, or water. Should they reflect the image of area?
- The urban fringe. Should it be a soft, landscape dominated edge or should there be a hard division between town and country?
- Should edges and pathways through the urban area be emphasized in line with the image?

A similar type of goal would be that relating to view protection. The usual wording in practice of view protection policies corresponds more to legal statements and standards than to goals and objectives. They should really stem from design goals, in particular, the image statement, if they are to have meaning. Otherwise, on what criteria are the buildings and landscapes to be seen and the positions from which they are to be viewed selected?

The goals describing **conservation priorities** also follow from an image statement. It is necessary to indicate, in broad terms, which historical period and forms should be conserved and what precedence, if any, should be given to each. Most buildings and landscapes acquire accretions over the centuries, and when they are restored the issue of what periods of building should be removed and what retained is a very real one. This will be the same for areas of towns as well as buildings. The necessity of making difficult choices is a reason why this type of goal should be stated in order

that the purpose of conservation in the area in question can be made clear. For example, is nineteenth-century industrial housing or 1930s suburbia an important feature of the history of the town? Are wide streets with tree planting dominant elements of the town whose retention should be a general goal? Even if there is no image statement, a conservation priorities goal will be necessary to provide a lead for answering these questions. If nothing is to be conserved then the goal statement should say so.

Design objectives and design areas

The goals will be fulfilled through the achievement of the **design objectives**. The design objectives are the most important part of a design plan. It is the objectives that will have the greatest significance in the negotiation of development. It is they that the public will be interested in for their own neighbourhood. It is the objectives that they may wish to challenge. There will be alternative ways of achieving each objective just as there will be alternative objectives for each design area. The range of alternative objectives will arise not only because there may be several ways of achieving each goal but also because the goals will be silent on many topics, and for many parts of the plan area, and the objectives will arise to fill the gaps. How, from among the range of alternative objectives, a 'preferred one' is selected, is discussed towards the end of this chapter. For the moment the discussion is concerned with the generation of alternative objectives.

The objectives will be determined by the interaction of the:

- design goals;
- existing physical form;
- existing land-use policies;
- existing and forecast development pressures; and
- degree of neighbourhood identity felt by residents and other users.

Design goals may not be fulfilled in equal measure throughout all of the plan area. Statements of objectives must be expected to vary spatially within the plan area. It is in the nature of urban design that it deals with arrangements of buildings and spaces laid out within the visual range of a walking human being. It

Figure 3.2 The result of not seeing the road as a design area
To the right, the turn of the century terraces front and enclose the street and incorporate mixed uses. To the left, the 1960s terrace houses present their blank ends to the street. They are set back behind an open space which has little obvious use and which removes the sense of enclosure

is, of course, possible that a specific arrangement may repeat itself over a very wide area but this fact does not detract from the essential point: design objectives may be necessary for subdivisions of the plan area, sometimes quite small areas. Areas to which a **design objective** applies will be termed **design areas**. They will be determined by the interaction between the goals and the existing physical form in the context of existing land-use policy and will reflect the variation in the possibility for fulfilment of the goals within the plan area.

It has been stressed that the design goals should apply, albeit variably, to the whole of a plan area. It then follows that the design objectives, and therefore the design areas, should cover the whole of the plan area. This may mean, in practice, that many design areas have a *laissez-faire* or open-ended objective. The point is that such objectives should be stated. The full set of design areas will be termed a **design area structure**.

Judgments concerning the desirability of retaining or encouraging certain physical forms will necessarily carry implications for the intensity of control. When a spatial variation in the level of intervention is proposed, ideally by a goal statement, then design areas

will emerge to distinguish between those parts of the plan area where strict control is envisaged, those parts where there will be more freedom for individual households, small shops and small businesses to redevelop within their plots, and those parts where more unconstrained development would be expected.

The way in which the design areas can emerge from the interaction between the design goals and the existing physical form and land-use policy can best be illustrated by taking an example from urban conservation. Let us suppose that there is a goal for a town to conserve its heritage from the industrially generated development of the mid-nineteenth century. Where areas of housing or factories from this period occur we would expect to see design areas created with conservation objectives. (If for the same town there was no such goal, then these same areas would be absorbed into adjoining ones.) As other periods or forms were identified within the conservation priorities then so the corresponding design areas would emerge.

If diversity is desired this should be so stated in the same manner as the seeking of character and identity. It stems from the very nature of control and negotiation that there will be topics for which nothing is said and on which the goals and objectives are therefore

25

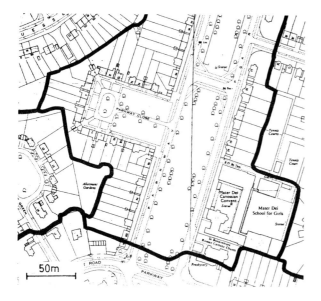

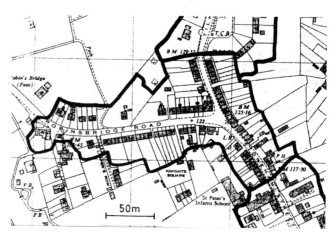

Figure 3.3 Examples of design area boundaries
Notice how they follow the ends of the back gardens, surrounding all the built form that encloses the road. Where there is a change in the urban form that may require a different design objective, the boundary crosses the line of the road to allow the start of a new design area. © Crown copyright

silent. Genuine negotiations imply that many (most?) items will be left for the parties other than the planning authority to propose or to dispose. This means, in urban design terms, that developers should be left free to pursue their own ideas within the planned context. This could allow, however, either **diversity** or **uniformity**. To remain silent is not the same thing as encouraging diversity. Diversity can be enforced, *in extremis*, by not permitting one new building to be the same as another nearby.

The boundaries of design areas

In most cases, the greater part of the land covered by design areas will conform to uniform land-use categories such as housing, shopping, industry. However, it is the edges of these areas where design objectives can be most important. Following from the arguments of Lynch,[7] edges and pathways should be seen as features that matter in design terms. The boundaries of the design areas will not necessarily be the same as those used in conventional land-use plans. Generally speaking, such plans tend to deal in parcels of land of uniform land-use and to make use of transport corridors, such as roads, railways, and landscape

features, such as parks and rivers, as boundaries of these parcels. Having defined the land-use subdivisions, the temptation is then to devise policies for these pre-set areas. The problem is where do the area definitions come from? From what principles are they derived? Are their boundaries sacrosanct? In practice they present obstacles to the formulation of urban design policy. Roads are used as boundaries whereas they need to be seen as townscape features.

Figure 3.2 shows the effect of not seeing the road as a design area. On one side there is an existing terrace form creating the appearance of a street while, on the other side, a housing estate has been designed with no thought to its contribution to the function or aesthetics of the street. Similarly, urban parks are, to a large extent, defined by their edges and surroundings which should be seen as part of the total design. It is proposed here that subdivision of plan areas should be derived from the interaction between the existing physical form and the overall goals, as are the design objectives. The boundaries of the design areas would, therefore, be dependent on the goals and objectives adopted. They would not be fixed for all time but be subject to revision as the plan and, in particular, the objectives are revised. They may occasionally coincide with existing neighbourhood and land-use parcels but this will not necessarily be the case.

Some types of design area will emerge from the goals dealing with general design principles. The need to see buildings and spaces in relationship to each other requires that design areas reflect the occurrence of different morphological types. Figure 3.3 shows a design area for a formal area of urban open space and for a major road in a large village. Note from each example where the boundary has been drawn. It passes through the private, rather than the public, space enabling the buildings defining the public space to be included in the design area. This is not to say that the private space is not important in design terms (it most certainly is) but that the intervention of the public authority in controlling design is justified more in, and is more appropriate to, the public realm than the private.

One especially important design principle is that of encouraging a variety and interaction of land-uses. Design goals cannot be fully realized within uniform land-use allocations such as 'residential', 'commercial', 'industrial' and 'educational'. Their use and literal interpretation in development plans leads to unsatisfactory consequences for urban design. Design areas provide a way forward. As they do not necessarily relate to land-use parcels they can be a vehicle for specifying the mix of uses appropriate to different localities. Objectives can convey the interplay of, say, housing, workshops, offices and shops that is sought. As this mix varies from place to place then so new design areas can be drawn.

It has been suggested previously that a range of alternative objectives should be proposed for each design area and a choice of one made from them. It has been mentioned that for any given goal there may be a range of objectives consistent with it and this range may vary from place to place. There is a potential difficulty here in that, as the boundaries of the design area relate to the objective, what happens to the boundary if different objectives are chosen? The answer is that, in practice, the only likely change is that the boundary may disappear as the design area merges with adjacent areas sharing the same objective. For example, within a large residential area of undistinguished character there may be a smaller area of greater quality. The design area for the residential area as a whole may merit alternative objectives ranging from conservation (unlikely) to a flexible open-ended approach (likely). The quality area may generate a similar range of choices but with conservation more likely than a minimalist approach. If both the areas end up with the same objective then the boundary between them effectively disappears. If not, it stays and is unlikely to be affected by other considerations.

Content of design objectives

What will be the likely content of the design objectives? Because of the almost infinite variety of local circumstances, can any order or structure be perceived so that content can be discussed and examples found? An initial difficulty is that there is no fixed vocabulary for describing the urban and rural environment. True, there are a large number of words that can and are used but their meaning is far from being constant and can vary between persons and contexts. **Form** and **style** are obvious examples. Whereas it is almost impossible to avoid their use they are not subject to precise or fixed definitions. This limitation applies to an even greater extent to terms relating to aesthetic impressions. An attempt is made here to start on the road to the development of a suitable terminology. However, this almost impossibly ambitious task cannot be accomplished within the confines of this book. All that can be done is to lay a foundation on which, hopefully, later work can build.

It is proposed that different design objectives should reflect degrees of intervention by the planning authority. Terms are needed that can express the physical implications of this variation. Rather than take solely a legal or procedural starting point the approach notes the concerns of the users of the environment. Local people often protest at new development and may even, on some occasions, welcome it. They are sensitive to definite changes in their surroundings both from functional and aesthetic points of view. Do these alterations resolve themselves into distinct types according to the degree of change and do these types correspond to categories used by professionals?

These questions can be examined by use of examples. The most productive will be those that employ urban forms about which a wide variety of views are commonly held, ranging from total demolition and redevelopment to careful preservation. We will take late-nineteenth-century villas and semi-detached houses, late-nineteenth-century terraced housing, and 1930s semi-detached housing. These are

27

(a)

(b)

(c)

Figure 3.4 Degrees of redevelopment – Park and Victoria Roads, Barnet
Park Road south side a
Park Road north side b
Park Road western end showing recent infill c
Victoria Road some original features d
Victoria Road some recent alterations e

(d)

(e)

forms that were built on a large scale in Britain and as estates which possessed their own overall urban design characteristics. Figure 3.4 shows a number of views of Park Road, Barnet, on the northern edge of greater London. In Figure 3.4a we see semi-detached houses from the late nineteenth century and as infill from the 1930s. The inter-war houses are marginally less bulky than their predecessors but have approximately the same building line and ridge height to the roofs. Their front entrances all face the road. The principal deviation from the original design of both periods is the paving of many of the front gardens by the residents to allow for access and parking. In spite of the different designs of the dwellings the experience of the urban form by the residents and the general urban design principles appear to be the same for both types.

(a)

(b)

(c)

(d)

(e)

(f)

Figure 3.5 Degrees of redevelopment – terrace houses in
Chelmsford
Baddow Road a
Baddow Road b

Upper Bridge Road c
Arbour Lane d
Primrose Hill e
Arbour Lane f

The opposite side of the road, shown by Figure 3.4b, presents a great contrast. The remnants of a line of nineteenth-century villas are squeezed between twentieth-century blocks of flats. The building lines and roof ridge heights are again the same but almost every other characteristic of the housing of the two periods is different. The bulk of the twentieth-century structures is substantially greater; the density of dwellings is greater; the dwellings are flats not houses; the roof design is different; the original plot boundaries have disappeared, communal gardens have replaced private and vehicles are accommodated at the rear rather than the front of the structures. Although all the dwellings have main windows facing the road, the 1980s flats have no front entrances on that side. In short, there has been within the same land-use category a significant change in both scale and function. It is these changes that tend to excite the public in this type of example. The stylistic and decorative changes have a small impact by comparison.

This is not to say that matters of style and decoration are not significant, just that they were not the principal urban design considerations in the case discussed. It can be noted in passing that the stylistic integrity of the original villas is in marked contrast to the appearance of the 1980s blocks. Such an issue becomes important when buildings of equivalent scale and function are being compared and when a high value has been set on the aesthetic qualities involved.

Infill, either in the 1930s as shown in Figure 3.4a or by the more recent houses illustrated in Figure 3.4c, can similarly replicate features of the original overall form while failing to reproduce any of the style. The roof lines, building lines and house types are the same but the treatment of entrances, garages and windows shows a different approach. It is neither reproduction nor original design but a stage in-between. At the end of Park Road is Victoria Road. The late-nineteenth-century house in the centre of Figure 3.4d has retained almost all of its original features. An intention to keep it in this condition would represent one extreme of a range of conservation objectives. The end-of-terrace house next door has not been conserved to the same degree, although many original features (such as roof and windows) remain. Its neighbours, shown in Figure 3.4e, have been altered to a greater degree but not to the extent that the integrity of the overall form has been lost.

Figure 3.5a shows similar houses in Baddow Road, Chelmsford, which exhibit a considerable degree of alteration. Note that a terrace form, with building line parallel to the road and windows and door looking out on to the street has, nevertheless, been maintained. Individual homes and gardens are still present. The alterations correspond to concept of **personalization** as set out in *Responsive Environments*. Similar personalization can be found further along the same road, as shown in Figure 3.5b, but with the **mixed uses**, another possible design objective. Figure 3.5c shows another street in Chelmsford where, although more respect for the appearance of the surviving terraces has been shown, there has also been twentieth-century infill in the shape of a block of flats. As in Park Road, Barnet, the building line and maximum roof height has been maintained but the bulk, shape, number of storeys, dwelling type, parking arrangements and plot boundaries are totally different. Figure 3.5c shows more recent flats, this time with same number of storeys and roof shape as the nearby terraces but without entrances facing the road and with communal lawns at the front. Figure 3.5e shows another recent block of flats more cunningly disguised as terrace houses. The appearance of individual houses is simulated. True reproduction of the terrace form, however, requires true houses and not flats as shown by the row of small dwellings illustrated in Figure 3.5f. Clearly there are degrees of adherence to what might be called terrace form and these could reflect different levels of intervention and alternative design objectives.

The same kind of pawtern emerges when we examine examples from the 1930s. Gidea Park on the eastern edge of Greater London is a noted suburb of this period. Examples of houses within it are shown in Figure 3.6. The house shown in Figure 3.6a, is in a derivative of the *moderne* style and has survived almost intact. The planting, but not, unfortunately, the garden wall, is also in period. To maintain this house as it is would imply an objective of strict conservation. Small alterations which do not affect the shape, bulk or relation to the plot and road can, nevertheless, result in the loss of the original decorative style. This can be seen in the houses on the opposite side of the road, shown in Figure 3.6b, which have lost their original *moderne* features.

To allow this while retaining the original suburban form represents a different intention. Further down the road from the houses shown in Figures 3.6a and 3.6b is the one shown in Figure 3.6c which was originally of identical design. Its decorative style, bulk and width

(a)

(b)

(c)

(d)

Figure 3.6 Degrees of redevelopment – 1930s houses in Gidea Park
Original *moderne* a
Loss of original features b
Substantial alteration c
Contemporary infill d

have been dramatically altered. Nevertheless, in spite of this considerable degree of personalization, it remains a house on its plot facing the road with the same building line and roof style as its neighbours. The contemporary pair of semi-detached houses shown in Figure 3.6d possess the same suburban form as their neighbours, with entrances, main windows and gardens facing the road on the same building line. However, the decorative treatment and roof style are different and there has been a marginal increase in depth and height, effectively adding an extra storey. What we see in these illustrations is four alternative design objectives reflecting gradual departures from the original 1930s design concept while retaining at every stage elements of a common form. (Further consideration of changes to a 1930s estate can be found in the discussion of the Avenues section of Chelmsford in Chapter 4.)

Standard forms of objective

The discussion of the examples suggests that it is possible that the almost infinite variety of design

31

objectives can be reduced in practice to a limited number of standard types. These standard types could form a template for the use of practitioners when preparing design plans and when developing design policy generally. They would also be useful for structuring the elements of the **four-way split**. They are alternatives that can be generated by considering firstly the different levels of intervention and, secondly, by identifying the different qualities desired within these levels.

Suggestions for standard alternatives are set out below. They are arranged in ascending order of controller intervention.

1 Minimum intervention

As it is assumed that a land-use plan exists, a truly **non-plan** approach is not possible. Another limitation on a purely *laissez-faire* objective is that pursuit of an objective for one design area may affect, say through visual intrusion, the achievement of one for an adjacent area. For these reasons we must talk about **minimum** rather than **non**-intervention. Referring back to the aims of the methodology, we must be wary of confusing intentions and results. This is a form of null objective which is silent on the aims of potential developers who may, and no doubt will, have their own objectives. The performance criteria will specify constraints on their activities to prevent interference with the fulfilment of goals and objectives for other design areas.

2 Height and bulk envelope

Here the objective focuses on the effect of buildings massing together, such that the whole form meets a desired shape, but is silent on what is desired within this envelope. The performance criteria and control procedures will define such matters as building lines but care should be taken to distinguish them from the objectives. Too often the objectives, particularly the aesthetic ones, are concealed when height limitations and building lines are imposed. Thought should be given to the desired overall shape of development, and it should be consistent with the area-wide goal. The desire for views of landmarks will require height objectives that result in height restrictions; imposing entrances will require encouragement of height within

uniform building lines; transport objectives will impose their own requirements and the general design principles may point to certain requirements regarding uniformity of provision. Where the design principles encourage stylistic goals (such as **regional identity**) a subdivision of this standard type of objective can be made according to the distinction set out above in relation to the types of goal.

3 Morphological control and personalization

The issue that is most likely to give rise to public reaction is one on which most land-use plans are silent. This is the redevelopment of existing urban areas where plots are aggregated, road layouts added to or revised, and buildings replaced. This may involve the replacement of small buildings by large ones and an increase in density for residential areas. If it is the policy of the planning authority to increase the density then this will certainly have urban design implications. It can be argued that density control should be the province of land-use plans, as it was for towns in Britain during the 1950s and 1960s. However, as argued in Chapter 2, density controls (and plot-ratio controls?) may form part of planning control but they should be seen as distinct from design control. The urban design objective should lead to the density specification rather than seeing density as a means of control. The link between density and urban form is a policy issue and should lie within the province of the land-use plan. Densities are averages and permit different morphological types within the areas to which they apply. What is meant by a morphological type? Urban morphology has its origins in the work of geographers and is important as a means of classifying urban form in a way which would permit a synthesis of the types of buildings, spaces and plots. As such it is a powerful tool for exploring the historical evolution of urban form and tying it in with legal, economic and social forces. Examples of morphological types are house and garden forms (with terrace, semi-detached and detached subforms) and street forms which contain parallel blocks of buildings enclosing linear public space. What is needed is a distinction between an objective that retains the morphological type and one that does not.

The first two types of standard objective (minimum intervention, height-bulk envelope) do not necessarily conserve the existing form and are consistent with redevelopment that aggregates plots and changes street patterns. The objectives concerned with conservation set out below aim both to preserve the existing plot boundaries and infrastructure and control change within plots. We can also have an objective which aims at preserving the existing form while encouraging diversity and individual initiative within plots. There is a difference between, say, redeveloping an area of houses and gardens as flats and maintaining this form while allowing extensions to houses as residents choose. The same distinction could apply to shops. The redevelopment of a street of small shops as a large supermarket is a different objective to the retaining small shops while encouraging choice and variety in shopfronts. The latter type of objective will be termed **personalization within plot**.

Not unexpectedly, there are difficulties with this concept. One is how the existing form is to be defined. Another is friction between neighbours. Many questions of the merits of house (or shop or office) extensions are not so much a concern with wider planning issues as the resolutions of disputes between neighbours. A distinction between disputes on the aesthetics of building appearance (for example, colour, materials, shape of roof) and problems such as alleged loss of light or privacy is helpful here. The latter could apply throughout the plan area, derived from the design principle goals, and expressed as regulations within the performance criteria. The aesthetic judgments, including whether to pursue uniformity or diversity, will be left to householders. This objective suggests that the planner should not intervene unless there are strong reasons for safeguarding the essential interests of the community other than aesthetic ones. Where such personalization is not permitted the objective will come within the **conservation** category below.

But what of new development on 'green field' sites or on sites where the existing buildings have been completely demolished? It may be the case that pursuit of a particular style is not to be enforced but neither is height and bulk limitation thought a sufficient control. What is required is a particular urban form. The objective should specify a particular morphological type. Examples would be the terraced housing form described in the discussion above and the case of buildings dominated by landscaping, often known as **arcadian** form. The latter is commonly associated with low-density residential developments of detached houses.

4 Specific form and style

Guidance is obviously clearer where there is a precise objective and we move to this with the objective of specific form and/or style. The distinction is made here between **form** and **style** and this is important. By specific form we mean here a morphological set that conforms to a particular design philosophy or vernacular expression, often associated with a particular historical period. Style is used here to refer to the decorative surface treatment of building and landscapes, similarly arising from aesthetic philosophies, vernacular expressions and economics of materials and similarly associated with historical periods. Most **forms** come with **styles** attached as both may spring from the same economic and social forces and aesthetic principles. Obvious examples are the classical forms of the late eighteenth century in northern Europe (known as **Georgian** in Britain) and the British **Regency** style and, less obviously, the residential areas, for both middle and lower classes, associated with the nineteenth-century industrial city.

In the twentieth century there has been a tendency to apply anachronistic style to contemporary form. The addition of neo-Georgian and neo-Regency motifs to standard late-twentieth-century housing is a controversial matter exhibiting a divorce between popular taste and critical professional judgment. However, mixing style and form is not necessarily a 'bad thing' as can be seen from the adaptation of a neo-classical style to garden city form in Welwyn Garden City and a neo-vernacular style to the same form in Letchworth new town.

This objective can be combined with that of **conservation**, as set out below, when there is an existing urban form that is to be conserved and extended in the same form and style. If the existing physical environment is not to be conserved then it will be gradually adapted by incremental redevelopment to the desired form and style.

5 Conservation

The objective of conservation is to retain, enhance or rediscover those aspects of the existing physical environment that have historical significance or are otherwise highly valued by the public. The problems involved in stating a conservation objective lie in the identification of the desired qualities and making the distinction between those aspects of the built form that are essential to them and must, therefore, be preserved, those that should be enhanced and those that may be altered or even dispensed with entirely. The distinction between objectives, performance criteria and procedures is important here. As with the other standard types, the consideration of level of intensity of control helps to clarify matters.

The following alternative types of objective are suggested and are set out in descending scale of preservation:

(a) exact period piece – every detail contributes to the aesthetic and historic quality and there is a presumption in favour of preservation;
(b) all significant buildings to be retained, along with road layout and major landscape features; spaces between buildings to be retained; however, there is silence (or diversity is encouraged) with regard to building details;
(c) as (b) but spaces not necessarily retained; new buildings replicating existing form encouraged.

There are clearly many variations on the above types. The role of the objective is to reflect the preservation/redevelopment balance which can then be specified more precisely in the performance criteria.

This discussion of the standard forms of objective is not intended to be prescriptive in the sense of saying that the objectives must always fall into these categories. Rather, it attempts, by categorizing the types of objective, to examine and illustrate what they should refer to and how they would fit within the overall methodology. Additional categories and subdivisions could have been described and examples will now be discussed that show more refined types of objectives developed to apply to local circumstances. At all times it is the general approach set out in the methodology that is important. Although it may be expected that practitioners will find it helpful to refer to standard types it would be counter-productive for them to do so rigidly.

Performance criteria

It can be held that the distinction between the goal and the objective is that the objective is sufficiently precise in its formulation for it to be known when it has been achieved. This implies that some criterion exists which will determine fulfilment of the objective and that this criterion can be clearly stated. However, there are also more pragmatic grounds for the use and development of such criteria. They can provide a useful, perhaps essential, means of understanding and defining what is meant by a specific objective. This is particularly true if the objective contains words such as **character** which, while conveying a general impression, lack a precise meaning. In addition, the argument that is central to this text, that potential developers should know exactly where they stand, comes into play forcefully here and requires that the intention expressed in the objective be represented in measurable physical terms. In other words, elements such as buildings, roads, and vegetation, with approximate sizes, must be used. The criteria must allow for a possible variety of ways of fulfilling an objective but must, nevertheless, make clear the circumstances in which the planning authority will be (or must be?) satisfied.

Performance criteria may be necessary but how can they be generated in practice? The following-step-by step approach is set out as a practical aid:

1. Set out initial thoughts on the meaning of the objective.
2. Draw outlines, termed here **exploratory diagrams**, of some examples of development consistent with the objective in both two and three dimensions and apply approximate dimensions.
3. Test the sensitivity of the initial statement by varying the objects and dimensions within the drawings noting what is essential to the objective and what violates it.
4. Express the resulting range of dimensions of buildings and landscapes as written regulations.
5. Sift out any superfluous regulations or those that should more properly belong under the **control procedures** heading.

Firstly, we can examine the example of **arcadian form**. The objective considered will be:

• to create a new residential area of detached houses in arcadian form.

The list of initial thoughts is as follows.

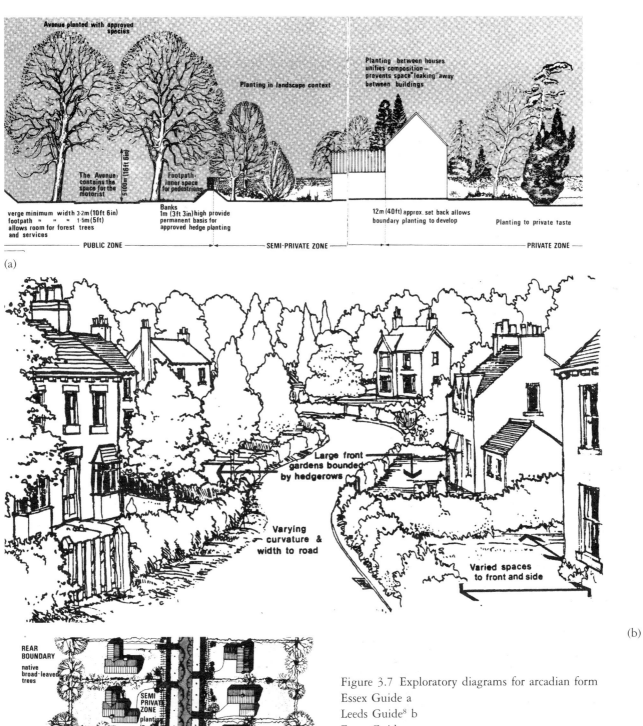

(a)

Avenue planted with approved species

Planting in landscape context

Planting between houses unifies composition — prevents space "leaking" away between buildings

The Avenue contains the space for the motorist

Footpath: inner space for pedestrians

verge minimum width 3·2m (10ft 6in)
footpath " " 1·5m (5ft)
allows room for forest trees and services

Banks 1m (3ft 3in) high provide permanent basis for approved hedge planting

12m (40ft) approx. set back allows boundary planting to develop

Planting to private taste

— PUBLIC ZONE — — SEMI-PRIVATE ZONE — — PRIVATE ZONE —

(b)

Large front gardens bounded by hedgerows

Varying curvature & width to road

Varied spaces to front and side

REAR BOUNDARY
native broad-leaved trees

SEMI PRIVATE ZONE
planting in lands

PRIVATE ZONE
exotic planting

PUBLIC ZONE
avenue planting

ISLAND specimen trees

(c)

Figure 3.7 Exploratory diagrams for arcadian form
Essex Guide a
Leeds Guide[8] b
Essex Guide c

- Landscape is dominant over buildings, in other words, trees are higher than buildings.
- A house and garden form is implied. Non-residential uses could be accommodated as long as the outward appearance of a residential area is maintained.
- There should be back and front gardens.
- Dwellings (or the equivalent) should be visibly detached.
- Road should be dominated by planting, especially trees.
- Low density is implied by the adoption of the arcadian form but it is not its origin.

Density could be expected to vary between different design areas exhibiting arcadian form. Just as many of the **policies** contained in design guides could be said to represent **objectives, standards** or **procedures,** so some of them could be held to be equivalent to the **exploratory diagrams** referred to. Examples can be found in relation to the **arcadian** form example and are reproduced in Figure 3.7. They are representative more of attempts to understand and explain arcadian form rather than merely to set standards.

The suggested written performance criteria are as follows:

- Conformity to the objective will occur if the following minimum conditions are fulfilled:
  - buildings normally have two principal storeys and do not exceed three storeys;
  - there is a minimum of one tree per plot higher than all the buildings on that plot;
  - grass, or other planting, cover at least half of each plot;
  - houses (or equivalent) are at least 30 m apart front to front and back to back and 5 m apart side to side;
  - buildings are at least 5 m from the front, 10 m from the rear and 2 m from any other plot boundary;
  - front gardens extend to at least 4 m;
  - trees, hedges or bushes are planted within a 2 m strip at the boundary to the road.

Examples based on nineteenth-century terraces, 1930s semi-detached houses and contemporary industrial estates can be found in Chapter 4.

Advice on achieving the objectives

The making of positive suggestions by planning authorities on ways in which an objective might be fulfilled, without placing limits on the range of design solutions, is a topic that has been neglected. Correctly used and interpreted, this is, of course, the role of a design guide. However, in spite of their excellent intentions, guides have not necessarily been structured for use in this manner in that their advice has been mixed together with objectives, standards and control procedures. Constructive suggestions may be welcomed by builders, save time for the development control staff, and leave the way open for imaginative contributions from architects. Some British planning authorities provide helpful leaflets giving advice on stylistic details and building materials for urban conservation, even to the extent of listing suppliers. For a particular form and style, books may be the best source of suggestions as they can cover the underlying principles, and their range of application, at some length. Clearly, if Regency, Georgian or Gothic Revival styles are being considered there are many books that can give a rigorous account of the details. It is therefore, likely that a design plan could refer to information of three types:

- design guides, correctly interpreted;
- leaflets setting short tips on styles and materials;
- recommended source books.

Examples can be suggested for the types of urban form discussed in this chapter:

- For the arcadian form, examples can be found within the Essex design guide. A typical and informative illustration from it is reproduced in Figure 3.8.
- For the late-nineteenth-century terrace housing the process of strict conservation can be aided by leaflets on style and materials, including addresses of suppliers. There are also several books on the appropriate styles, the most notable being Muthesius, *The English Terraced House*[9] and Johnson, *Your Victorian House*.[10]
- For 1930s suburbia there is an ideal book, Barrett and Phillips' *Suburban Style*.[11]

Development control procedures

It is essential that means should be distinguished from ends and therefore the control procedures should be set out separately from the intentions of the plan. There may be several ways of implementing a chosen objective even, as is the case here, when we may be considering incremental change as the inevitable vehicle. Opportunity should be given for the imaginative use of legal instruments. Urban design is affected by the law on such topics as property, highways and pollution in addition to that strictly concerned with town and country planning. Distinguishing between elements requiring direct control from those where openness and flexibility may be appropriate is, therefore, also important. We end up with the same kind of split suggested for the design plan methodology as a whole:

• What are the means by which the planning authority envisages the objectives will be implemented?
• What legal and administrative procedures will definitely be employed?
• What possible, but not compulsory, procedures are suggested for the potential developer?

As contrasting examples, we can take the pursuit or retention of arcadian form and the strict conservation of 1930s or nineteenth-century areas. The **arcadian form** is simplest. If we are dealing with a design area that has either little existing built form, or where no conservation objective applies, the implementation will result from construction initiated by a developer and will be dealt with by standard development control procedures under the appropriate legislation. The only additional procedure might be the use of a tree preservation order. A short statement to this effect would be included in the design plan. As an example of non-compulsory procedures, the planning authority could include a suggestion of the desirability of planning agreements by which the developer would agree to pay for landscaping, especially tree planting, within the plot over and above the minimum required by the performance criteria, and also, within the public domain, for roads, footpaths and open spaces. For the strict conservation of the late-nineteenth-century terrace housing and 1930s suburbia more detailed procedures would be required.

In the English context, the control of the details listed in the performance criteria would require an Article 4 direction[12] that would remove all exemptions for permitted development. If such a direction were to be made permanent then the consent of central government, in the person of the Secretary of the State for the Environment, is required. It is argued here that the design plan for the methodology proposed would greatly assist in obtaining such consent by placing it in a more systematic context than applies at present. If such consent is not forthcoming then the complete achievement of the objective by legal controls may not be possible. The planning authority would have to fall back on exhortations, pressure from neighbours and amenity societies (in which it could take an active role) backed up by the following legal instruments (in addition to the normal powers under the Town and Country Planning Acts):

• conservation area designation, which would provide demolition control;
• tree preservation orders.

In England, the local authority making these orders may also be the one who controls the maintenance of the highway and its planting. Some aspects of the achievement of the objective would, therefore, be a matter of inter-departmental co-operation. It is suggested that this process would benefit from being made more explicit in the authority's own documents.

Preparation, participation and adoption

So far we have not considered who would prepare and who would approve design plans, largely because it has not been central to the argument. It is also a matter which will be subject to much variation according to the systems used in both different countries and regions of countries. Nevertheless, as it is of understandable concern to practitioners, it is important to set out briefly how the methodology proposed above would tie in with the general responsibilities of local politicians and the officers of the local planning authority.

The basic model, common to systems in many countries, is:

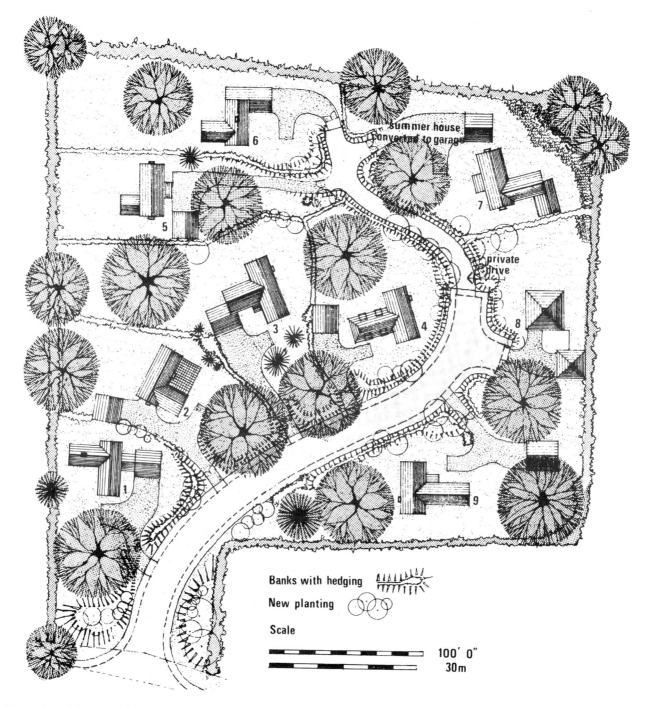

Figure 3.8 Advisory information – arcadian form from the Essex County Council Design Guide for Residential Areas

- officers draw up proposals;
- local politicians agree to the publication of the proposals;
- public reaction is received and considered;
- officers make revised proposals to politicians;
- politicians give final approval.

If this sequence of events is adapted to the methodology for design plans as set out above, the sequence of events as set out below is generated. It is described according to the British context but this should not affect the general applicability of the points suggested.

1. Planning officers for a local authority propose design goals to the planning committee (or equivalent body of local councillors).
2. If approved, the design goals are publicized and comments from the public received.
3. The officers revise the goals as necessary and put them before the committee.
4. If the committee approves the design goals, the officers prepare the design area structure, plan-wide objectives, and alternative objectives for each design area and put them before the committee.
5. If agreed by the committee, the officers publicize these proposals and prepare public participation displays for selected (or, possibly, all) design areas depending on the significance of the proposals. The public are invited to respond by means of questionnaires.
6. On the basis of the response to the public participation exercise, the officers prepare a revised design area structure (if necessary) with recommended objectives for each design area.
7. The committee approves the design objectives.
8. The officers prepare the full design plan, including the suggested ways and means of achieving the objectives.
9. The full design plan is publicized and comments received.
10. The committee receives the full design plan, with comments from the public and gives its final approval.

This procedure is set out on the assumption that the design plan is not incorporated within a statutory land-use plan. There are arguments for and against incorporation of a design plan within a legal development plan and the answer may, in practice, be determined by local circumstances. The argument for incorporation derives from the need of prospective applicants to know where they stand and to have some certainty that the planning authority's position will not be subject to rapid change. It would also enable the policies to be challenged through formal objection at the approval stage and the authority would, by the same measure, have the confidence that, once approved, the design plan was safe from challenge. On the other hand, it could be argued against incorporation that the subject matter of design control is different from land-use plan content and needs to operate in a situation where flexibility in negotiation is an essential requirement. In addition, the revision and continuous evolution of policy which involves a fair degree of detail is better achieved in a more informal context. However, many would argue that land-use and design issues are not all separate and development plans should reflect their interrelationship. It could be said that it is the land-use plan procedures that need to change.

As with all plans, the design plan will require periodic revision, possibly continuous updating. It is most unlikely that one could remain relevant for more than five years without revision, given the level of detail it would contain. The design area concept may, in fact, be very helpful in facilitating the partial updating of the plan. Some design areas may experience many changes and may require frequent revision while others (for example historic areas with a require of strict conservation) may be fairly static and require infrequent revision. A procedure is suggested whereby the committee can approve revisions to the statements made for individual design areas without changing the overall framework of the design plan. If such an approach is not adopted, then complete revisions of all design objectives should be undertaken every five years. It will also be necessary to undertake quinquennial reviews of the design goals.

There can be longer or shorter versions of the proposed procedures, depending on how much public or politician involvement is required, and failure to obtain committee approval at any stage would generate additional feedback loops. If it seems a somewhat elaborate process, then it should be borne in mind that a lot of the plan content, especially control procedures, will already exist, it is just that they are not normally written down, debated and subjected to formal approval. What is being said here is that there is a role in design control for the officers, the local politicians and for public participation, whatever the detailed arrangements may be, and that these roles can be played out in public.

Summary

To develop a method for the preparation of design plans, the different aspects of the problem were disaggregated while bearing in mind always the overall intention of facilitating negotiation between parties and serving the public at large.

A four-way split was proposed, distinguishing between:

- goals and objectives;
- performance criteria;
- advisory information;
- control procedures.

It was proposed that plans, and thus goals, should apply to the whole plan area. The effects of the goals would, nevertheless, be manifest in different ways in different parts of the area. This would in turn result in the variation of the objectives from place to place. From this observation developed the simple but powerful concept of the design area.

The use of design areas would create many advantages, especially the following:

1. They would enable design objectives to be applied to roads (and streets), squares, parks, rivers (including their banks) and all other urban and landscape features. They would thus be compatible with townscape analyses.
2. They would permit the intensity of control, i.e. the degree to which the planning authority exercises its powers of intervention, to be varied from place to place within a proper framework. It should be stressed that this is not a compulsory feature and the design area technique remains just as valid without it.
3. They would permit the specification of a mix of land-uses and enable this composition to vary from locality to locality.

The suggested approach would enable both the public and local politicians to become more involved in the process of local planning in general and urban design in particular. The objectives could occur in a number of standard forms depending on the degree of intervention and the qualities to be encouraged or conserved. Such standard forms could be used to structure the performance criteria, advisory information and control procedures.

This method has been put forward not as a rigid programme or set of rules but as a rule-of-thumb to assist people in structuring their thinking and making clear their intentions.

Notes and references

1. Essex County Council (1973) *A Design Guide for Residential Areas*, Chelmsford: Essex CC.
2. This is represented by the best in current British practice as is shown by Dept. of Environment (1991) *Best Practice in Development Plans*, London: HMSO. What would be termed a goal here would correspond to 'aims' as used in Harlow, p. 33, and 'principles' as used in Hounslow, p. 36.
3. J. V. Punter (1990) The Ten Commandments of architecture and urban design. *The Planner*, 76(39), 10–14.
4. HRH the Prince of Wales (1989) *A Vision of Britain: A Personal View of Architecture*, London: Doubleday.
5. Anonymous (1988) Urban design, Tibbalds offers the Prince his Ten Commandments. *The Planner*, 74(12), 1.
6. I. Bentley *et al.* (1985) *Responsive Environments: A Manual for Designers*, London: Architectural Press.
7. K. Lynch (1960) *The Image of the City*, Cambridge, Mass.: MIT Press.
8. Leeds City Council (1982) *Residential Design Aid Site Potential.*
9. S. Muthesius (1982) *The English Terraced House*, New Haven and London: Yale University Press.
10. A. Johnson (1991) *Your Victorian House*, Newton Abbott: David & Charles, 2nd edn; see also J. Marshall and I. Willox (1986) *The Victorian House*, London: Sidgwick & Jackson.
11. H. Barrett and J. Phillips (1987) *Suburban Style: the British Home 1840–1960*, London: MacDonald.
12. Article 4 of the *Town and Country Planning General Development Order* (made under the Town and Country Planning Act 1971 ss. 24,78).

Chapter 4

THE CHELMSFORD CASE STUDY

To illustrate the application of the ideas set out in Chapter 3, a fully worked example was developed for the town of Chelmsford in Essex. A preliminary version was published in 1990 in the form of a short book and an article.[1] The proposals put forward were entirely the author's own and did not necessarily represent the views of the Essex County or Chelmsford Borough Councils. Its purpose was limited to the illustration of the arguments and it was not an attempt to plan the town in a professional sense. If the same exercise were to be undertaken by the planning authority, then the results could very well be different for a number of very good reasons. Chelmsford was chosen because of its convenience and familiarity to the author and also because it did not present many special cases in terms of heritage and design. In addition, its planning history and its position on development plans and design policy guidance illustrated many of the points made in Chapter 2.

The town and its design policies

Chelmsford lies 30 miles north-east of London on the main rail and road route to East Anglia. Although of Roman foundation, it remained a comparatively small town until the expansion of the electronics industry in the 1940s. Ever since, it has been a prosperous and rapidly expanding town, with extensive housing, road and retail provision under construction almost continuously during the 1970s, 1980s and 1990s. Although it possesses some historic buildings and spaces dating from medieval times onwards, they are not extensive and Chelmsford could not be characterized as a historic town. On the contrary, its public image is one of being nondescript, to say the least. This is not to say that there are not parts of the town with existing, or potentially realizable, character but, in the public mind, there is certainly room for improvement in both its appearance and amenity.

The case study related to the urban area of Chelmsford as shown in Figure 4.1. This lay within the much larger area of Chelmsford Borough Council which incorporated the surrounding towns, villages and countryside. The Borough Council was the planning authority for most local matters although some remained the prerogative of the Essex County Council and the central government. At the time of writing, a *Borough Plan*[2] which covered the whole Borough, had been prepared and was awaiting final adoption. This plan was subject to the provisions of the *Essex County Structure Plan*[3] but the latter did not have significant design implications. Prior to the adoption of the *Borough Plan*, the only statutory development plan that had covered the whole of the Chelmsford urban area had been the obsolete *Town Map* which was a land-use plan only and contained no discussion of wider policy or design guidance. This had been prepared under the 1947 Town and Country Planning Act with the first version appearing in 1957 and the first revision in 1964. A second revision was approved by the central government in 1976 although the new development plan system, incorporating structure and local plans, had been introduced five years earlier with the 1971 Act. The first local plan under the 1971 legislation did not appear until 1984 when the *Town Centre Plan*[4] was adopted. However, the 1984 plan did not cover all of the urban area, as can be seen from Figure 4.1. Interestingly, in terms of the argument of Chapter 2, this left the town centre without an up-to-date local plan during the early 1980s and a very large area of the

Figure 4.1 Plan area boundaries for Chelmsford. (Courtesy of G.I. Barnett & Son Ltd)

town surrounding it without any current local plan at all until 1995. Nevertheless, control decisions affecting design and detailed appearance were made throughout the Borough, including the 'plan-less' areas, for all of this period. In 1974 the Borough had adopted the provisions of the Essex Design Guide[5] as supplementary guidance but this did not form part of the statutory development plan.

Very few local areas were covered by specific design policies. As Figure 4.1 shows, outside the town centre plan area only Springfield Green and the Chelmer Village housing estate, a largely 1980s development, were covered. The conservation area for Springfield Green was a clear example of the minimalist approach to information criticized in Chapter 2 as the document consisted just of a map showing the area boundary. No other information was available. The Chelmer Village planning briefs[6] were site and time specific and this development had been completed by the early 1990s. The *Town Centre Plan* was not, in the main, concerned with design issues, as opposed to broader land-use considerations. It is difficult, however, to draw a clear line between the two nor should such a hard and fast distinction be made. The Plan had a 'Conservation and Townscape' section and parts of the 'Transport and Recreation' sections touched on matters of built form and landscape. The *Town Centre Plan* policies made no reference to sub-areas, apart from the environs of the Cathedral. Conservation area boundaries were shown in the *Proposals Map* but there was little in the way of positive statements about specific parts of the town centre. The *Borough Plan* of 1995 covered the whole administrative area of the Council. With regard to the urban area of Chelmsford town, it incorporated and built upon the policies of the *Town Centre Plan*. Urban design was covered by a dedicated chapter entitled 'Built Environment'. This set out five **objectives** which were the equivalent of the **design goals** recommended here. They were:

(i)   to create conditions that will help improve the quality of life in the Borough;
(ii) to improve the image of the Borough;
(iii) to ensure that all new development is of the highest possible standard;
(iv) to create a clear sense of place;
(v)   to protect and enhance the Borough's archaeological, historic and architectural heritage.

It is interesting to compare them with the goals set out in the author's 1990 study:

(a)   The image of the town should be enhanced and greater identity provided;
(b)   given the strategic location of the town, its identity as perceived by travellers to and from it should be emphasized;
(c)   all remaining items of architectural and landscape heritage should be valued;
(d)   selected examples of urban form from all periods of Chelmsford's development should be valued.

Objectives (ii) and (iii) were clearly the equivalent of goal (a). Objective (v) was the equivalent of goal (c). The idea of 'heritage', as with many urban design terms, can be a difficult concept. What were the features considered worthy of protection and enhancement? Although the goal must be general, the **policies** in the plan should have made the criteria clear. They would have been the equivalent of the **objectives** recommended in Chapter 3. In fact, those in the plan did not add a great deal to (v) and limited its area of operation to conservation and listed buildings. Protection and enhancement of buildings outside these categories were not envisaged and specific criteria, such as historic period, were not given. The suggested goal (d) was of interest here as it does provide at least one criterion. Using it, we would expect at least one example, hopefully more, to have been retained from each period of history. Chelmsford's past record of preserving its heritage has not, unfortunately, been a good one. The boundaries of conservation areas were tightly drawn and, as late as the early 1990s, certain unlisted historic buildings outside of them were still being demolished. With regard to (ii), there was nothing in the **policies** and accompanying text that provided a definition, or even a description, of the existing 'image' or what 'sense of place' might be required. Goal (b) made some suggestions regarding approaches to the town, given Chelmsford's location on main rail and road routes, but this could, admittedly, be a difficult proposition to achieve.

The significant point in (iii), the one that distinguished it from the normal run of 'motherhood' statements, was the use of the strong words 'all' and 'highest possible'. If they were to be taken literally, achieving this goal would indeed be a tall order. There was little evidence of such a goal having been achieved

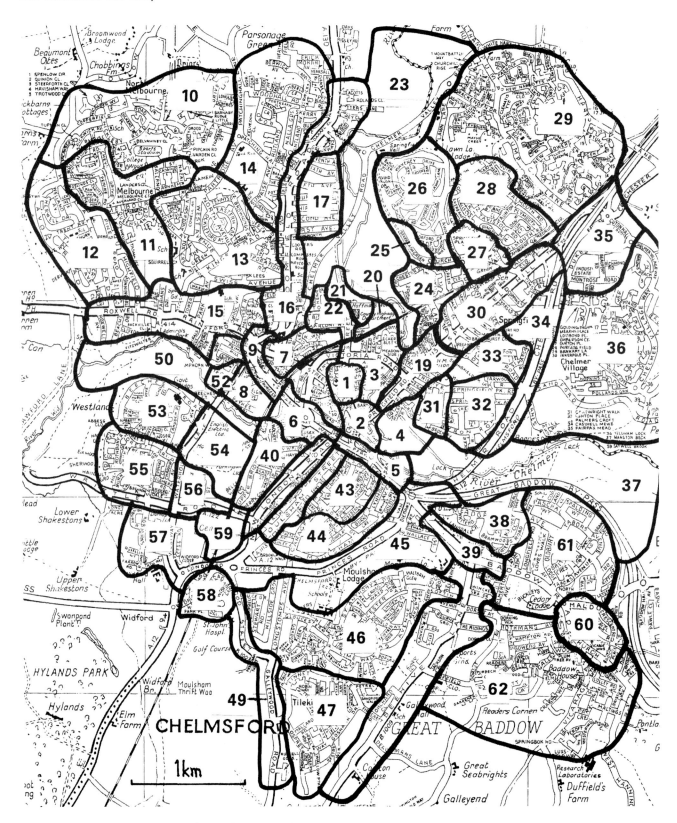

Figure 4.2 A design area structure for Chelmsford. (Courtesy of G.I. Barnett & Son Ltd)

in the town in the past. The word 'all' implied a uniformly high standard without variation from one part of the Borough to the next. Could this be achieved without detailed design guidance? The policies in the plan give some detail on home extensions and much detail on garden size but little elaboration on any other aspect of design, save for the colour and texture of building finishes. They state that, the development 'should normally be sympathetic to the vernacular range of Essex materials'. The Essex design guide was not referred to in any way, presumably because a revised version of the ageing 1973 document had not appeared by the time of the plan's preparation.

The design area structure

The 1990 study used the goals referred to above and applied them to the existing physical form. The goals were by nature general and could be interpreted in different ways and to different degrees in different parts of the town. In particular, goal (d) implied that a selection of examples for conservation should be made. This was done and a design area structure was worked out and this is shown by Figure 4.2. For each design area a range of alternative objectives was generated and these were set out in full in an appendix. It was recognized that if a political decision was taken to select the same objective in design adjoining areas then they would coalesce, thus creating a simpler structure than that shown in the figure. Two areas, Springfield Road and the Widford Industrial Estate, were examined in detail and are also included in this chapter.

In the 1990 study, adoption of a specific design philosophy was not made one of the goals. Instead, the question of whether or not the development should follow a design guide was used as a means of generating alternative objectives as described in the discussion of standard objectives in Chapter 3. The *Borough Plan* proposes no overall design philosophy and does not mention the Essex guide. To incorporate a comprehensive policy on the lines of the precepts of, for example, *Responsive Environments*[7] would clearly have constituted a major departure. It could be argued that to have maintained the existing form of, say, the Springfield Road, as discussed in this chapter, would have been to incorporate many of the principles such as perimeter

blocks, mix of uses, and a certain degree of personalization and richness. However, it was in the industrial, major retail and entirely new development, where there may be little continuity with the past, that the adoption of design principles became an important issue.

Bearing these points in mind, it was decided to base the Chelmsford case study described here on the following features of the 1990 study:

- the goals;
- the design areas;
- the two design areas taken as examples, Springfield Road and the Widford Industrial Estate.

In addition, the Widford example would incorporate more discussion of alternative design principles, and an additional example, an area of inter-war private housing, would be added. This additional example would draw upon the discussion of the design control of 1930s housing in Chapter 3, providing contrasting material to the other two.

The Avenues – an area of 1930s housing

Background

On the east side of the main road leading north out of Chelmsford is an area that has been given the name The Avenues for the purposes of this book. This name arises from the rather uninspiring choice of road names from First Avenue through to Seventh Avenue. Its location is shown in Figure 4.2 (area 17) and its boundary and layout by Figure 4.3.

It was built in the 1930s as a speculative housing development and the form and style were typical of the period, comprising semi-detached houses, all with long back gardens, laid out along a uniform building line in a series of straight roads. Figure 4.4a shows views of parts of the area where the original appearance of the houses, road and landscaping has been largely maintained. Throughout the greater part of the area the original houses and plot boundaries remain, although the buildings have, in most cases, been subject to varying degrees of alteration and extension. Figure 4.4b shows a loss of original detail without significant changes to the overall shape of the dwelling

Figure 4.3 Map of 'The Avenues' design area. © Crown copyright.

while Figure 4.4c shows alterations without much respect for the original form or style. The area experienced sporadic infill during the 1950s, 1960s and 1970s, with vacant sites being built on and groups of houses being demolished and their site redeveloped. This new building has largely been confined to isolated pockets. One is illustrated by Figure 4.4d which shows a row of 1970s semi-detached houses that have replaced a smaller number of the originals. They keep to the original height, shape and building line envelope and front the road, albeit by porches with side entrances. The style, however, is completely different not only with regard to the porches but also the roof shape, open plan front gardens and overall detailing.

Generation of objectives

The relevant goal leading to the designation of this design area was:

d selected items of urban form from periods of Chelmsford's development should be valued.

Alternative objectives could arise depending on the degree to which this goal should be applied. The goal implied that at least one area of private housing from the 1930s should be retained. If The Avenues was not chosen then the area would be open to redevelopment. If it was, then the question of the degree to which it would be appropriate to conserve the urban area would arise. What aspects should be preserved and what altered? From these considerations five different scenarios were developed resulting in the following five alternative design objectives. They are arranged in decreasing order of intervention:

1. strictly conserve the 1930s form and style;
2. conserve the original 1930s form but not the stylistic detail;
3. maintain the suburban form but with personalization by residents within their plots;
4. encourage redevelopment within the precepts of the Essex design guide;
5. encourage redevelopment with minimal restrictions.

Performance criteria

For each of the alternative objectives, performance criteria were generated on the lines set out in Chapter 3.
  Objective 1 would be fulfilled if:

1a. minor alterations are made to buildings and planting;
    1a.1   original roofs, doors, windows, front garden

(a)

(b)

(c)

(d)

Figure 4.4 Views of 'The Avenues' design area showing degrees of redevelopment a–d

walls, and gates are retained or reproduced in facsimile with (or close approximation to) the original material;

1a.2 replacement of later period roofs, doors, windows, garden walls and gates are in the period applicable to the period style;

1a.3 walls and hedges for front gardens do not exceed 1.2 m in height;

1a.4 front gardens have a minimum of 60 per cent soft landscaping; no hard standings for vehicles, other than at the approaches to garages occur within front gardens;

1a.5 back gardens have a minimum of 70 per cent soft landscaping;

1a.6 existing trees are retained, or replaced from list of species popular in the 1930s;

1a.7 satellite dishes do not appear on the front (road facing) elevation of the house;

1b major alterations to existing buildings and planting;

1b.1 1a.1–1a.7 above apply;

1b.2 all existing period structures are retained;

1b.3 extensions to houses do not exceed 20 per cent by volume, and reproduce the period style;

1b.4 the roofs of extensions are of the same, or approximately the same, style, proportion and materials as the original;

1b.5   extensions to have doors, windows, and wall renderings and facings reproduced to conform to the period style, if possible in the same materials;

2. all existing houses from 1930s are retained;
3. all trees are retained;
4. road paving, verges and lampposts (where possible) are maintained in the original style.

Objective 2 would be fulfilled if:

1. for infill:
   1.1   all existing plot boundaries are retained;
   1.2   where larger existing vacant sites are to be subdivided, new plot boundaries have the same dimensions as adjacent plots (35–50 m 3 8–15 m);
   1.3   new dwellings are detached or semi-detached (or, exceptionally, a three-dwelling terrace);
   1.4   dwellings are 10 m from front of plot;
   1.5   no back-land development;
   1.6   roofs are hipped and tiled;
   1.7   buildings occupy no more than one-third of the plot by area;
   1.8   all houses have two principal storeys, not more than three storeys in total, and a minimum width of 6m;
   1.9   front and rear elevations have large windows to the principal rooms on each floor, the front windows being of a bay design;
2. extensions to houses do not exceed 20 per cent by volume, and reproduce the period style;
3. existing plot boundaries are maintained;
4. existing building lines are maintained.

Objective 3 would be fulfilled if:

1. plot boundaries are maintained;
2. dormers are allowed but no third storey;
3. there is no back land development;
4. there is no subdivision into flats.

Objective 4 would be fulfilled if:

1. development does not exceed the height of the existing houses;
2. development accords with the principles of the Essex design guide;
3. there are new access roads to development but no new major roads.

Objective 5 would be fulfilled if:

1. land-use remains residential;
2. highway standards are as in the design guide supplement.[8]

Advisory material

For an objective of conservation, advisory material of a good standard was available in the form of books, one of which, Barrett and Phillips' *Suburban Style*[9] is highly recommended. For an objective of redevelopment, design guides were appropriate sources, although only the Essex guide applied to the locality in question. The author, with some artistic assistance from others, has also contributed drawings indicative of the possible consequences of the objective being fulfilled.

Objective 1

Figure 4.5a shows how the area could look under strict conservation with the preservation of most of the original features, similar to the situation shown in Figure 4.4a. Barrett and Phillips' *Suburban Style* should be consulted by potential developers.

Objective 2

Figure 4.5b shows changes to the view in Figure 4.5a consistent with this objective. While the original shapes remain, stone cladding, plastic windows and satellite dishes are in evidence. Figure 4.4b shows alterations well within the compass of this objective.

Objective 3

Figure 4.5c shows personalization of the same dwellings as in Figures 4.5a and 4.5b, consistent with this objective, even if the mock medieval extension may be somewhat unlikely in practice. The alterations shown in Figure 4.4c would be well within the intentions of this objective.

Objective 4

Figure 4.5d shows a view of development in the same road consistent with this objective. The new

Figure 4.5 Design objectives for 'The Avenues' – advisory illustrations
Strict conservation a
Original form but not stylistic detail b
Maximum personalization c
Redevelopment within design guide d
Maximum freedom for redevelopment e
1970s development in Chelmsford f

development shown in Figure 4.4d would not meet this objective as it does not meet the Essex design guide's goal of **regional character**.[10]

Objective 5

Figure 4.5e shows redevelopment of the same road consistent with this objective. The illustration is based on development that has occurred elsewhere in Chelmsford since 1970. A more extreme example, which includes garages facing the road, is shown in Figure 4.5f.

Development control procedures

Following the argument of Chapter 3, the legal procedures should be distinguished from the rest. The implementation of objective 1 would require the use of an Article 4 direction,[11] or if consent for this from the Department of the Environment was difficult to obtain, conservation area designation and tree preservation orders would be necessary. For the achievement of objective 2, no special powers would be necessary as all the alterations shown in Figure 4.5b, for example, would be within the range of development permitted under the *General Development Order*.[12] Approval of extensions and garages and the refusal of permission for more substantial development would be carried out within normal planning control powers and procedures. For objective 3, planning authorities would refrain from exercising their powers regarding the appearance of buildings while, at the same time, using them to prohibit development involving the amalgamations of plots and the construction of flats. For objectives 4 and 5 the planning authority would refrain from exercising all its powers. Development in pursuit of all the objectives would be subject to the land-use provisions of the *Borough Plan* and the highway standards of the County Council.

Upper Springfield Road

Background

The Springfield Road was part of the main London–Colchester Road until by-passed in the 1930s. This by-pass was itself by-passed in the 1980s but the

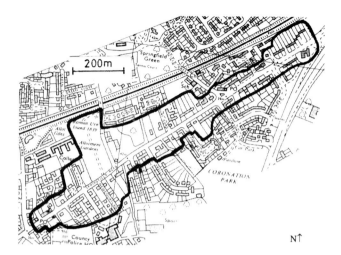

Figure 4.6 Map of the Upper Springfield Road design area. © Crown copyright

Springfield Road remained a main entrance to the town centre from the Colchester direction. Its location is shown in Figure 4.2 (area 40). The plan of the road is shown in Figure 4.6. During the nineteenth century it acquired isolated groups of Gault brick terraces in a simple but elegant style as shown by Figure 4.7a. From the turn of the century onwards the dominant morphological type became one of large villas in their own grounds with substantial trees and shrubs as shown by Figure 4.7b. Over the last 30 years many of the plots of the villas have been redeveloped to create closes with houses, bungalows or sheltered housing as shown in Figure 4.7c. This figure illustrates well the likely fate of most areas of large houses in their own grounds in urban settings when subject to unrestricted pressure for redevelopment. It demonstrates the need for the explicit consideration of alternative design objectives. That such development is not a necessary outcome is demonstrated by Figure 4.8c which shows infill from the 1970s in the same form and style as the nearby nineteenth-century villas.

Generation of objectives

Three of the overall goals for the town determined the selection of this road as a design area. They are:

'(a)   given the strategic location of the town, its identity as perceived by travellers to and from it should be emphasized;

(a)

(b)

(c)

Figure 4.7 Views of the Upper Springfield Road design area showing degrees of redevelopment a–c

(b) all remaining items of architectural and landscape heritage should be valued;

(c) selected examples of urban form from all periods of Chelmsford's development should be valued.'

The boundary chosen in the light of the general objectives is shown in Figure 4.6. It included not only those buildings fronting the road but all those that have been developed within the original plot boundaries and could have a functional or aesthetic impact upon the highway. No prior information was available on the views of residents, councillors or amenity societies on the gradual redevelopment of the road. On the assumption of the goals set out above, the following range of alternative objectives arose from consideration of the interaction between the goals and the physical form:

1. Strictly conserve the form and style of the existing nineteenth-century villas and terraces while encouraging the redevelopment according to either objective 2 or objective 3 of areas built in later periods.

2. Extend the nineteenth-century villa form and style to the whole road.

3. Extend the nineteenth-century terrace form and style to the whole road to create a street. Mixed uses encouraged.

4. Encourage comprehensive redevelopment in an imposing contemporary form and style to emphasize the entrance to the town.

5. Encourage comprehensive redevelopment according to the precepts of the Essex design guide.

6. Encourage redevelopment with minimal restrictions.

Performance criteria

The following criteria were derived from each objective:

Objective 1 would be fulfilled if:

*   no villas, terraces, walls or outbuildings from the nineteenth century are demolished;
*   all trees are retained;
*   all gardens and open spaces are retained as such;
*   windows, doors and roofs are retained or replaced in the original style and materials;
*   extensions do not amount to more than 20 per cent of

the original building and have the same style and detailing as the original;
*   buildings from later periods are replaced by development that accords with the criteria for objectives 2 or 3 and reproduces the nineteenth-century style and detailing; (i.e. for objective 3: windows, doors and door cases of wood in the existing simplified classical style).

Objective 2 would be fulfilled if:

*   redevelopment is at the same number of buildings per hectare as the existing villas;
*   the buildings are detached with a minimum separation of 10 m;
*   the buildings have red brick outer walls and pitched roofs in red tile or slate;
*   the buildings do not exceed the height of the highest trees;
*   the buildings are of two or three storeys, not counting dormers;
*   the buildings are set back at least 10 m from the edge of the road;
*   brick walls mark the boundary with the road;
*   vehicle access is via a private drive to each building.

Objective 3 would be fulfilled if:

*   the buildings are terraces with a maximum length of 50 m and normally two storeys in height;
*   the terraces are divided into separate properties each having a maximum width of 10 m;
*   the roofs are pitched with the line of the ridge normally running parallel to the centre line of the road;
*   terraces of length 40 m or more are broken at the centre by a property of three storeys with the ridge of the roof at right angles to that of the terrace;
*   the properties, especially their entrance doors, front the road;
*   the front of the property is normally 2.3 m from the boundary with the highway;
*   there are no dormers;
*   the outer walls are of Gault bricks or similar appearance;
*   the roofs are of slate or similar appearance.

Objective 4 would be fulfilled if:

*   the buildings have a minimum of three storeys and a maximum of seven storeys;
*   the buildings are in connected blocks of a maximum length of 60 m;

(a)

(b)

(c)

(d)

(e)

(f)

Figure 4.8 Design objectives for the Upper Springfield Road design area – advisory illustrations
Conservation of villa form and style a
Development in villa form b
Development in villa form c
Development in terrace form d
Development in imposing form e
Redevelopment within design guide f

- the blocks are set back from the edge of the highway by a minimum of 5 m and a maximum of 10 m;
- a recognizable and consistent style is applied to the facades;
- the treatment of planting, front access and boundary to the highway should all be consistent with the chosen style.

Objective 5 would be fulfilled if:

- development will not exceed three storeys;
- development will accord with the principles of the Essex design guide;
- there are new access roads to development but no new major roads.

Objective 6 would be fulfilled if:

- highway standards are as in the Essex design guide supplement.

Advisory information

Drawings of the type that would show the implications of the objectives were made. Figure 4.8a illustrates the possible appearance of the Springfield Road if objective 1 were to apply. The villa shown in Figure 4.7b has been maintained in a manner that would accord with this objective. Unfortunately it is not possible to show equivalent illustrations for the terrace form as, although no terraces as shown by Figure 4.7a have been demolished in recent years, neither have they been subject to detailed preservation or restoration.

Figure 4.8b shows the possible appearance of the road when redeveloped in the villa form according to objective 2. The buildings shown could be large individual houses or small blocks of flats. The comparatively recent villa in the Springfield Road shown by Figure 4.8c would be well within the compass of this objective. It could also be consistent with objective 1.

Figure 4.8d shows the possible appearance of the road if redeveloped at higher density to form a street with terrace houses. The form and style mimic the existing one illustrated in Figure 4.7a. Some premises could be shops, as is the case with the existing terraces.

Figure 4.8e shows blocks of flats constructed with the objective of creating an imposing entrance to the town. The style is reasonably modest but a more adventurous one would still be consistent with objective 4. Figure 4.8f shows redevelopment in the form of blocks of flats in a manner consistent with the Essex design guide. Figures 4.5d and 4.5e show development in accordance with an objective of minimal restriction and, as remarked when considering The Avenues design area, they are taken from actual examples in a nearby part of the town.

Development control procedures

Implementation of objective 1, strict conservation, would require an Article 4 direction if it were to be strictly applied to all alterations, such as changes to windows, doors and planting. Conservation area designation would be essential. Implementation of all the other objectives would not require the use of any special powers.

Widford Industrial Estate

Background

The Widford industrial estate is one of the principal industrial and trading areas of the town. It occupies a very significant site where the main road from London enters the urban area. Almost all the buildings date from after 1950 and some are of recent construction. Its location is shown by Figure 4.2 (area 57). The plan is shown by Figure 4.9. On the eastern half of the area are the Britvic and former Marconi buildings which form significant points of reference for people entering the town by road. It is difficult to refer to them as landmarks in the conventional sense. They are certainly not beautiful as can be seen from the view in Figure 4.10. It shows a former Marconi building, Elettra House, as seen from the London direction. Figure 4.11a shows the same building from Westway. The western half of the area, as shown by Figures 4.11b, has taken on a predominantly wholesale and retail function with car repair, car spares, and retail warehouse business moving in. Notable is the building shown in Figure 4.12 that was once a carpet retailers and is now a bowling alley. It also occupies a prominent position at the entrance to the town. Apart from a generally low building height there is little

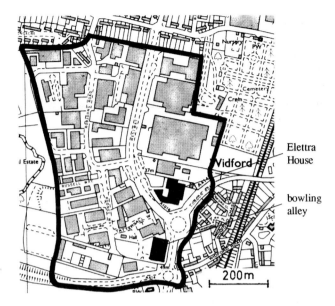

Figure 4.9 Map of the Widford design area. © Crown copyright

evidence of any positive planning control, or major design initiatives by the owners, in the whole Widford estate.

Design guidance in this situation is important not only because of the prominent position of the estate but also for the following reasons that apply to all similar areas.

- Manufacturing industry is declining both in its occurrence and in the space it requires for its activities. Land is vacated and allocations for future use are not taken up. The estates are increasingly dominated by warehouse, retail and leisure concerns. These uses are often characterized by large structures with prominent, sometimes garish, signs and colour schemes.
- The industrial, retail and warehouse uses all require access by heavy goods vehicles. The leisure and retail uses require extensive car parking. The consequent road and parking provision can result in unaesthetic and sometimes intimidating layouts. People without the use of a motor vehicle can find that access has been made very difficult.
- There is a pronounced lack of visual identity and consequent loss of legibility.

- There is confusion between public and private areas. Frontages to the highway are rarely created.
- The approach to landscaping, often introduced with the best of intentions, can aggravate the lack of enclosure without ameliorating any of the other problems identified above. In the case of Widford, its consists of wide grass verges along the line of the roads without any clear function.
- There is no provision for uses other than industry, retail and leisure. This results in a lack of amenities for employees and visitors, particularly for food and drink. Mobile snack bars appear to provide for this need and, by their very presence, advertise the shortage of permanent facilities, as can be seen in Figure 4.11b.

There is nothing inevitable about these shortcomings. Contemporary industrial buildings, particularly those of a **high-tech** style, can be visually appropriate and of a high architectural standard. As reference to the past can show, the industrial estates of the 1920s and 1930s, such as the Great West Road in London and the Slough Trading Estate, avoided many of the pitfalls referred to.

Generation of objectives

There is little of heritage value on the site no matter what aesthetic values are adopted. The relevant design goals are those of establishing the identity of the town via its entries and exits:

(a) the image of the town should be enhanced and greater identity provided;
(b) given the strategic location of the town, its identity as perceived by travellers to and from it should be emphasized.

Late twentieth-century manufacturing industry is a major part of the economic base of Chelmsford and part of its physical, as well as economic, form. Taking this fact together with these goals, it would lead to industrial estates being defined as design areas, particularly those in prominent positions. The Widford estate should therefore be a design area with the general objective of giving identity to the approach from the south-west. Alternative objectives within this could be deduced from this by considering variations

Figure 4.10 The Widford Industrial Estate from the London direction

(a)

(b)

Figure 4.11 Views from within the Widford Industrial Estate a–b

in the intensity of control: Four degrees of intervention were identified and are set out below in declining order.

- Promotion of an overall urban design philosophy. The Council may wish to intervene extensively, via design briefs or otherwise, to correct the design problems identified above.
- Promotion of a particular appropriate aesthetic. The Council may feel it is in the interests of the town as a whole to take a positive initiative and to encourage owners to adopt a particular style when the time comes to extend or redevelop their premises. Some particular architectural styles may be identified as more appropriate than others.
- Restriction on the overall height and bulk to within the existing limits. The Council may feel much sympathy with the arguments for freedom for developers but may be concerned to prevent any development of the site affecting other areas. It may wish to give freedom to the owners to pursue their own style of building but within the existing comparatively low height limit. It may also wish to conceal the less becoming buildings by means of extensive landscaping.
- Minimum intervention. It could be argued that industrialists and out-of-town retailers have an interest in creating a successful identity for their enterprises and it is from their actions that a prominent and relevant identity for the area would arise. Therefore, subject to regulations governing access for heavy vehicles and customers' cars, there would be minimal intervention on the part of the Borough Council as planning authority. The local plan provisions would apply but no industrial design guide.

Although there were many possible variations on these levels, for the purpose of this case study three major choices of objective could be identified:

1. encouragement of frontages to the highway, with rear parking and servicing, a mix of uses and amenities for employees and visitors;
2. encouragement of a particular aesthetic style;
3. maximum freedom for development.

Although pursuit of the first choice would be highly desirable, it is far from being the existing situation as can be seen from the illustrations. Attempts have been made in Essex[13] but it has been very much an uphill struggle. Whereas choice (3) is incompatible with the first two, choice (2) could, if desired, be combined with (1). It could also be resolved into many sub-objectives, four of which are set out below:

(a) Encouragement of a neo-vernacular style. Such an approach is becoming increasingly common for retail and wholesale premises in Essex and other parts of the country.
(b) Encouragement of a high-tech style. This could be held to be visually appropriate to Chelmsford's position as a centre of the electronics industry.
(c) Encouragement of traditional outward features. The guide for many retail, wholesale and business parks encourages designers to moderate their style in deference to popular taste while not being overly prescriptive.
(d) Landscape dominance. The public may be happy for little control to be exerted over the appearance of individual buildings as long as they can be largely hidden by a visually distinctive planting and landform.

Performance criteria

The following performance criteria were developed for the achievement of objective (1):

- buildings have their front entrances facing the road;
- buildings are a maximum of 10 m from the road (15 m in the case of objective (d), below);
- servicing facilities are to the rear;
- there is at least one permanent refreshment facility on the estate.

For the achievement of the stylistic sub-objectives of objective (2) we would have:

Objective (a), achievement of a neo-vernacular style, would be fulfilled if the buildings have:

- steeply pitched roofs with low eaves;
- one or two storeys;
- roofs of red tile;
- walls of red brick with wood cladding, where appropriate.

Objective (b), achievement of a high-tech style, would be fulfilled if:

- there was a minority of buildings taller than the others and rising to 30 m;
- variation in the cladding using metal, plastic and glass.

Objective (c), achievement of traditional outward features, would be fulfilled if the buildings have:

- a height of one to three storeys;
- brick outer walls;
- pitched roofs.

Objective (d), achievement of landscape dominance, would be fulfilled if:

- tree height exceeds building height;
- a minority of trees are higher than the others;

- the view of the buildings from the road is largely obscured;
- there is a variety of tree and bush types;
- a 15 m wide belt separating the building from the road with 5 m planted with trees and bushes and 10 m with grass.

Advisory information

The application of a neo-vernacular style to new buildings that are remote from traditional uses is illustrated by the case of the second-hand car auction premises at Boreham on the outskirts of Chelmsford as shown by Figure 4.12. This was the result of control exercised by the Borough Council when the car auction was moved from the original site near the centre of town. The result of applying this style to a hypothetical redevelopment of the bowling alley, as seen in Figure 4.13 is illustrated by Figure 4.14.

Figure 4.12 Motor Auction Building, Boreham, Chelmsford

Figure 4.14 Advisory illustration for the Widford Industrial Estate – neo-vernacular style

Figure 4.13 The Bowling Alley as seen from the Widford Roundabout

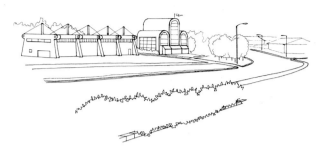

Figure 4.15 Advisory illustration for the Widford Industrial Estate – high-tech style

An example of how the application of a high-tech style to a hypothetical redevelopment of the former Marconi site shown in Figures 4.10 and 4.11a is illustrated by Figure 4.15.

An example of the application of limited traditional features to an otherwise modern structure is illustrated by a retail park in north Springfield, Chelmsford, shown by Figure 4.16. Applying this approach to the bowling alley site could produce the view shown by Figure 4.17.

The application of the landscape dominant approach to the view shown in Figure 4.13 is illustrated by Figure 4.18.

Figure 4.16 Traditional outward features – a retail park in Springfield, Chelmsford

Figure 4.17 Advisory illustration for the Widford Industrial Estate – traditional outward features

Figure 4.18 Advisory illustration for the Widford Industrial Estate – landscape dominance

It could be argued that the present appearance of the estate, as shown in Figures 4.10–4.13 approximates to a situation of minimum intervention. Only the roads and verges appear to result from any semblance of overall design.

Public participation

An important part of the argument has been that the design plans could facilitate greater involvement of the public in the control process. To illustrate this point a pilot public participation exercise was undertaken during the summer of 1991, sponsored by the local newspaper, the *Essex Chronicle*. Four large display panels were created and are illustrated by Figures 4.19–4.22. The first introduced the entire case study and the other three each showed five alternative design objectives for one of the design areas. The panel covering the Widford Industrial Estate contained photographs of the general views of the area, as shown in Figures 4.10–4.13, and the examples of development elsewhere in the town, shown by Figures 4.12 and 4.16. No other panel showed exact pictures of existing buildings, in order to avoid embarrassment or offence to residents, and the drawings shown by Figures 4.14, 4.15, 4.17 and 4.18 were prepared as illustrations. Nevertheless, these drawings were based indirectly on the actual buildings and locations. The panels were displayed in the atrium of the Essex County Hall for one week during September 1991. Passers-by were asked to fill in a short questionnaire which asked them to indicate which of the alternative objectives they preferred. It also asked them whether they thought that the Borough Council should carry out this sort of exercise and, if so, how frequently. Twenty-three people responded and the results are shown by Table 4.1. Given the small number of replies, and the fact that the respondents were not necessarily residents of the design areas in question, the exercise can be regarded as only a pilot study.

Table 4.1 Results of the Survey of 'The Avenues', 1994

Example 1, 'The Avenues'

Strict conservation of 1930s style	71%
Conservation of suburban character but not stylistic detail	4%
Suburban form with maximum freedom for residents	0%
Redevelopment within design guide	25%
Maximum freedom for development	0%

Example 2, Upper Springfield Road

Conservation area	52%
Maintenance of villa forms	22%
Street forms	13%
Imposing forms	9%
Redevelopment within design guides	4%

Example 3, Widford Industrial Estate

Encouragement of a neo-vernacular style	27%
Encouragement of a 'high-tech' style	9%
Traditional outward features	27%
Landscape dominance	37%
Maximum freedom for redevelopment	0%

Would you like to see this sort of exercise carried out for your area by the Borough Council?

All the time	73%
Sometimes	27%
Never	0%

DESIGN OPTIONS FOR YOUR AREA

Conceived by
TONY HALL

Anglia Polytechnic

This display demonstrates a means of involving members of the public in the control of the design of towns. It is about how things could be done and how, in particular, options could be put forward for people's choice.

1

What is the problem?

Like it or not, towns are in a constant state of change:
- open sites, small and large, are built on
- existing buildings are demolished and their sites, small and large are built over
- people extend and enlarge their houses, shops and factories

All of this is subject to planning control and development control is guided by planning policy, notably local plans and design guides. However, there is a lack of guidance on the detailed design of particular parts of towns:
- local plans are concerned with land use and are not design specific
- design guides, while important and useful, are very general in their application and are mainly residential in scope.
- detailed design briefs are aimed at major new development, mainly in town centres.

There is little advance information on what would be acceptable designs in, say, specified factory estates or outlying residential areas. Moreover, there is little sense of the pursuit of positive images for localities nor, alternatively, identification of where people could be allowed "to do their own thing". The result is that there is little opportunity for local people to make their views known in advance of a planning application being made and, consequently, disagreements surface at a later and more disruptive stage.

The Proposal

(a) There should be overall "design goals" for a town.
(b) Towns should be divided into "design areas". These would be based not just on neighbourhoods but also on prominent roads and open areas.
(c) Alternative "design objectives" should be drawn up for each design area.
(d) The views of the public should be sought on the alternative objectives.
(e) A preferred alternative should be adopted by the planning authority as its policy.

How do we get alternative objectives?

Alternative objectives can be generated from the answers to the following questions:
- Should there be very strict control or should there be a lot of leeway?
- Should the existing form and layout be retained or should developers be allowed to combine plots and build anew?
- Should a particular form or style be sought?

Some design goals for Chelmsford

It is suggested that the following goals would be useful additions to the policies contained in the Chelmsford Borough Council Town Centre Plan:

(a) The image of the town should be enhanced and greater sense of identity provided.

(b) Given the location of the town on major road and rail routes, its identity as perceived by travellers to and from it should be a particular concern.

(c) All remaining items of architectural and landscape heritage should be valued.

(d) Examples of urban forms and styles from all periods of the town's past should be selected for conservation.

These goals have been used to generate the design areas shown on this panel and some of the objectives within the detailed examples on the succeeding panels. However, some objectives have been obtained by using only selected goals and some by using none of them in order to illustrate their implications.

Suggested "design areas" for Chelmsford

The map below shows a possible division of the Chelmsford urban area into "design areas" made on the basis of a study of the characteristics of different localities and consideration of the goals opposite. Note that streets, roads and open spaces can all be treated as separate design areas. The use of design areas also enables the strictness of planning control to be varied from place to place.

The following design areas have been selected, as examples, to provide illustrations of the range of alternative design objectives in different areas and form the subjects of the accompanying panels:

About this display

This display forms part of work that is being carried out at the Anglia Polytechnic on the control of urban design and is the recipient of an Essex Chronicle bursary award which has financed the production of these panels. The research is being undertaken by Tony Hall, who teaches town planning at the Polytechnic, and stems from work he started while on sabbatical leave at the Joint Centre for Urban Design at Oxford Polytechnic. The research has no official connection with either Chelmsford Borough or Essex County Council. A full account of the work is available as a short illustrated book:

"Generation of Objectives for Design Control",

obtainable from:

Professional Services Unit,
Dept. of the Built Environment,
Anglia Polytechnic,
Victoria Road South,
Chelmsford, CM1 1LL. at £12.50 inc. p. & p.

Please give your opinion of the ideas in this display by completing the questionnaire supplied.

Figure 4.19 Public display panel 1 – Introduction. © Crown copyright

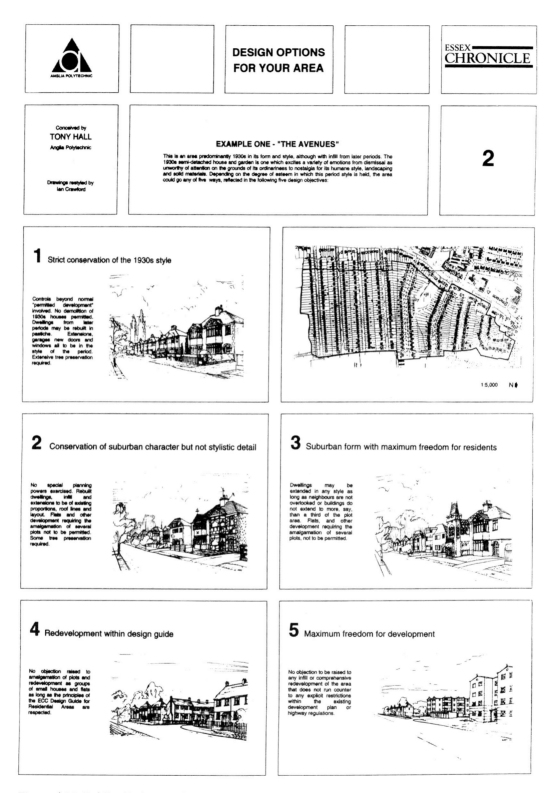

Figure 4.20 Public display panel 2 – 'The Avenues'. © Crown copyright

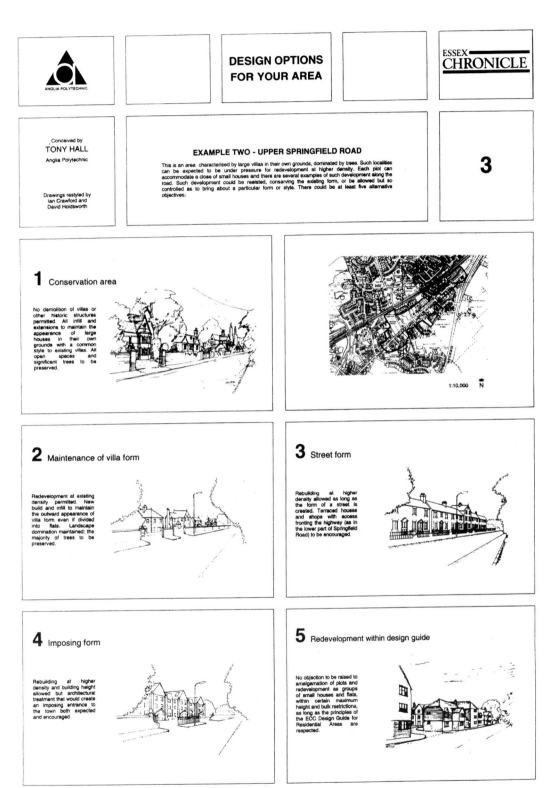

Figure 4.21 Public display panel 3 – Upper Springfield Road. © Crown copyright

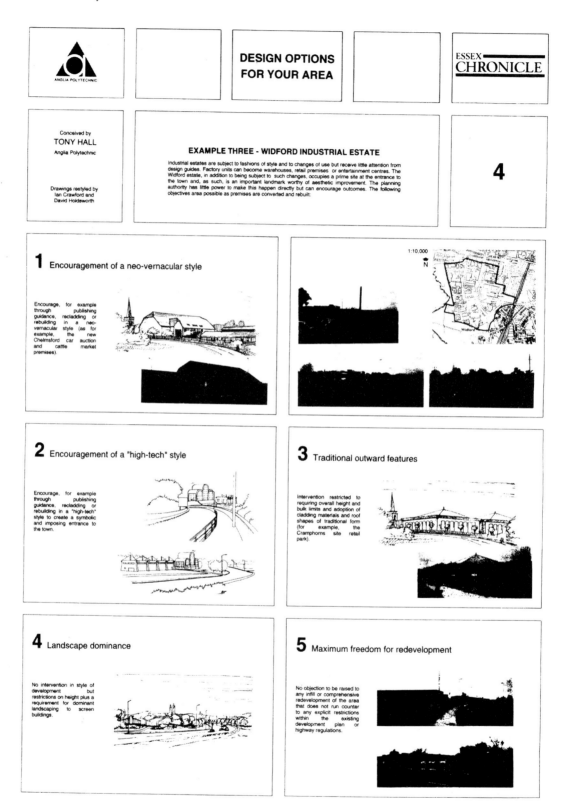

Figure 4.22 Public display panel 4 – the Widford Industrial Estate. © Crown copyright

Table 4.2 Results of the Survey of The Avenues, 1994

Preference for the Design Objectives

Strict conservation of 1930s style	52%
Conservation of suburban character but not stylistic detail	29%
Suburban form with maximum freedom for residents	6%
Redevelopment within design guide	3%
Maximum freedom for development	2%
No response	8%

Would you like to see this sort of exercise carried out by the Borough Council?

Definitely	53%
Sometimes	21%
No	11%
No response	15%

Nevertheless, some of the results were worthy of note. There was:

- no support for development with minimal restrictions;
- a preference for traditional and conservative form and style;
- a very clear preference for the strict conservation of 1930s semi-detached housing;
- a definite wish for the Council to carry out such consultations.

The survey also confirmed the general desire for such a consultation exercise to be carried out by the planning authority, with three-quarters supporting this as something that should occur on a regular or occasional basis. The results for the 1930s housing were the most dramatic and so a further investigation of 'The Avenues' area was carried out during 1994.[14] A sample survey of 7 per cent of the 900 households was obtained and a questionnaire on the same lines as the pilot survey was administered. The results are shown in Table 4.2. They confirmed the desire for the conservation of style. Eighty per cent sought it and nearly two-thirds of these wanted it strictly maintained.

This reaction by the residents of a 1930s housing area was remarkable; firstly, because such development is not normally the subject of conservation area designation and, secondly, because people were voting for restraint on their own freedom of action. A possible interpretation is that they would want to exercise their freedom if they saw their neighbours doing so but would, nevertheless, prefer them not to do so in the interest of maintaining the character of the area and the value of their property.

Summary

As this exercise has not been carried out by the planning authority, it has not been subject to the ultimate test of implementation. Nevertheless, the feasibility of the preparation of design plans has been demonstrated by working through the stages of formation of goals, design areas, objectives, performance criteria, advisory information, control procedures and public consultation. Examples of what a design plan could look like have been provided. Hopefully, practitioners will eventually carry out full-scale tests of design plans. In the meantime, some clues on their potential effectiveness can be obtained by seeking examples from current practice which parallel at least some of the recommended techniques. This is the purpose of the following chapter.

Notes and references

1. The book was A. C. Hall (1990) *Generation of Objectives for Design Control*, Chelmsford: Anglia College Enterprises; the article was A. C. Hall (1990) Generating design objectives for local areas: a methodology and case study application to Chelmsford, Essex. *Town Planning Review*, 61 (3), 287–309.
2. Chelmsford Borough Council (1993) *Chelmsford Borough Plan Deposit Draft*, Chelmsford: Chelmsford BC.
3. Essex County Council (1995) *Essex Structure Plan: Written Statement*, Approved Second Alteration, Chelmsford: Essex CC.
4. Chelmsford Borough Council (1984) *Chelmsford Town Centre Local Plan*, Chelmsford: Chelmsford BC.
5. Essex County Council (1973) *A Design Guide for Residential Areas*, Chelmsford: Essex CC.
6. Chelmsford Borough Council (1977) *East Springfield Planning and Design Brief*, Chelmsford: Chelmsford BC; and (1985) *Chelmer Village South Design Brief*, Chelmsford: Chelmsford BC.

7. I. Bentley *et al.* (1985) *Responsive Environments: A Manual for Designers*, London: Architectural Press.

8. Essex County Council (1980) *A Design Guide for Residential Areas: Highway Standards*, Chelmsford: Essex CC.

9. H. Barrett and J. Phillips (1987) *Suburban Style: the British Home 1840–1960*, London: MacDonald.

10. Essex County Council (1973) *A Design Guide for Residential Areas*, Chelmsford: Essex CC, p. 15, para. 3.4.1. Shown in this book by Figure 3.1.

11. Article 4 of the *Town and Country Planning General Development Order* (made under the Town and Country Planning Act 1971 ss. 24,78).

12. *Town and Country Planning General Development Order* (made under the Town and Country Planning Act 1971 ss. 24,78).

13. See for example, Essex County Council (1984) *South Woodham Ferrers: Western Industrial Area Design Brief*, Chelmsford: Essex CC.

14. R. Mabbitt (1995) *Structuring Character Assessment: a Case Study of 'The Avenues', Chelmsford.* Unpublished working paper presented to the Urban Morphology Research Group, University of Birmingham.

Chapter 5

EXAMPLES FROM BRITISH PRACTICE

Chapter 4 demonstrated that it was feasible to prepare a design plan but was not able to discuss its implementation. The method proposed is new and there has not been time to try it in practice and monitor the results. It was possible, however, to search for examples of the partial application of the ideas. In some cases planning authorities may have either followed some of the suggestions made in the earlier publications or have anticipated them. Although investigations in Western Europe and North America would certainly prove rewarding, because of limited resources the search was confined to British practice. What was looked for was:

- objective-driven plans in pursuit of urban design goals, not just the aesthetics of individual buildings;
- policies for locations outside historic and other sensitive areas;
- use of design areas or similar devices.
- Having discovered such examples, the question was whether such a policy framework aided implementation, particularly the day-to-day development control process.

As remarked in Chapter 2, British structure and local plans had not been seen by most planning authorities in the past as appropriate vehicles for detailed urban design policies. There was a lack of published design policies and frameworks that could contain them. Fortunately, recent evidence had shown a significant trend towards greater design content in British development plans. Starting from the sources cited in Chapter 2, the search progressed by word-of-mouth reference from planning authority to planning authority, supplemented by a manual search of the DoE Library in London. The greatest progress was made in locating those planning authorities that had, to some

degree, adopted a design area approach. One, Dacorum Borough Council, had explicitly adopted the recommended approach and produced a complete design area structure with design objectives for each town within its boundaries. In the event, more material was discovered than could be conveniently used and geographical limits had to be placed on the authorities described. Apologies are offered to those pioneering authorities who have had to be omitted.

It must be stressed that the work of the planning authorities used as examples in this chapter represents a selection of the best practice discovered. Any criticisms of them ventured here should not be seen as detracting from this. Similarly the omission of any planning authority does not imply substandard practice on its part, merely the practical limitations of the search and of space in this chapter.

The results of the search can be reviewed under three headings:

- conservation areas;
- areas of special residential character;
- areas of special landscape character.

Conservation areas

It was for conservation areas that most convergence with the argument of this book had originally been expected. There had been a clear public consensus on the need for design control for conservation and the historic fabric to be conserved was usually located in clearly defined areas with particular and explicit needs. Some conservation guides anticipated selected aspects of the argument. A particularly good example was that for the Queen's area of Belfast[1] which made a clear distinction between

The Riverside

This stretch of the Thames has an open aspect; not only does the river curve in both directions, but there is little built development on the opposite bank, and the buildings on Lonsdale Road and The Terrace are set back from the embankment. Unfortunately, the flood wall blocks the view of the river for anyone travelling by car, particularly in a south to north direction; however, this does give greater impact to the views which are available at either end, and those using the raised footpath have a better view than motorists do. The density of traffic, and its speed along this stretch, diminish enjoyment of the views, and the towpath below the wall, along The Terrace, is disfigured by jetsam and dumping. At the Lonsdale Road end, an unsightly area of concrete and grass encourages casual parking, including lorry parking, which blocks the river view and access to the riverbank.

The embankment wall itself is unattractive and monotonous, and does nothing to contribute to the 'seaside' feeling engendered by the tidal shoreline, the raised walkway, the open views and the architectural character of the terraces. Beyond Small Profits slipway the riverbank is wooded. North of the High Street junction it is appropriate to reinforce this character by further tree planting in Lonsdale Road, South of the High Street junction, where the shoreline narrows, a reinforcement of the 'seaside' character and public enjoyment and use of the river can be encouraged. Barnes Bridge, the

Station entrance and the White Hart pub are all a focus of interest but Barnes Bridge is marred by an unsightly hut at the abutment, the Station entrance is badly in need of improvement and the White Hart, although it has attractive balconies to the river, does not relate well to the towpath or make enough use of the adjacent area of riverbank. There are no features of interest or viewing points along the floodwall, and it would considerably increase the attraction of this area if small traditional lamp standards (as in other locations on the Thames) and viewing points could be provided.

Environmental Improvements

E 1 Lonsdale Road (north end adjacent to Small Profits slipway)

An area where the raised concrete ramp leading to the slipway meets a stretch of rough grass. Dumping and casual parking, including lorries, blocks views and access. (See also Project B4 in the Local Plan).

Re-design to confine parking to an area near the road. Define line of towpath to join existing paths. Extend tree planting. Encourage use of slipway and possibility of landing stage (see TRN 30).

E 2 Raised footway and flood wall, Lonsdale Road

Bare concrete wall and footway protected by steel railings of poor design and colour.

Repair and paint railings and investigate possibilities for improving their appearance.

E 3 Footway and flood wall, The Terrace

Wall is not of the same standard as the listed Bridge, and the area does not encourage pedestrian use.

Provide small lamp standards on top of wall, and/or investigate other possibilities for improving its appearance.

E 4 Barnes Bridge Station entrance

Building is neglected and a potential hazard to users, and needs restoration. (See also 13.8(10) in the Local Plan).

Liaise with Network South East to obtain improvements.

E 5 Towpath, between Barnes Bridge and White Hart PH

Towpath disfigured by litter and dumping, use spoilt by traffic noise.

Provide screen planting below wall and above towpath.

E 6 Barnes Bridge

Bridge needs painting. Ugly hut at abutment.

Encourage Network South East to paint to an agreed scheme. Encourage removal, or provide planting screen.

Opportunity Sites

OS   Area adjoining White Hart PH, The Terrace

Outside use of pub poorly provided for, and spoilt by traffic proximity and noise.

Encourage owner to provide usable outdoor space (at low tide) and screen to road.

Figure 5.1 Extract from the Barnes Green Conservation Study, London Borough of Richmond

character analysis, problem analysis, the role of development control and design guidance, similar to the **four-way split** introduced in Chapter 3.

The publications of the London Borough of Richmond-upon-Thames were of high quality and particular interest. The guidance for Richmond's conservation areas showed a robust approach. As can be seen from the example for Barnes,[2] shown in Figure 5.1, a distinction was made between problem analysis, detailed proposals, and development control procedures. However, welcome as the approach was, it shared with most other conservation documentation a reluctance to state explicit objectives for the area in question. A clear idea was given of what the Council wished to do in order to prevent people damaging the character of the area, in particular the identification of small-scale improvements. However, the nature of the character that was being conserved was not made explicit. It could be held that this was a minor matter because the character of some of the areas in question was obvious. However, it would be difficult to sustain this position for more controversial, say 1930s, areas or when dealing with applicants who lack knowledge or sensitivity for architectural history. It is more likely that the reason for this was the absence of a detailed character analysis together with the general lack a convenient and effective language for making such statements, over and above that provided by townscape notation.

More examples of superior guides could be quoted but these initiatives do not reflect the arguments made here for the application of design control to urban areas of less than outstanding quality and, therefore, the need to make explicit the appropriate degree of conservation in different circumstances. One procedure that does appear to do this, however imperfectly, is based on the notion of 'areas of special residential character' which are discussed in the next section. Apart from these special concepts, conservation areas that refer to outstanding historic places do not illustrate the breadth of the argument and it is not, therefore, intended to discuss them further but to pass on.

Areas of special residential character

The most extensive use of quasi-design area approaches apart from obviously historic areas was found to be the use of **areas of special local character**. This term was applied almost exclusively to residential areas dating from the late nineteenth century to the present day. They all shared an objective of conservation but its interpretation was found to vary in degree from area to area according to local circumstances. They had their origin in development pressures and planning restrictions that had combined since the 1950s to create intense pressure for the redevelopment of existing urban areas at higher densities. During the late 1980s reaction to such development began to grow generally within the country and it acquired the name 'town cramming'. In many, if not most, suburban areas there had been significant resistance to this process and representations were made by local politicians and organizations for the maintenance of what the residents saw as the existing character of their areas.

This feeling could be seen as connected to the moves in both public and professional tastes towards a greater degree of conservation of the built environment and the adoption of neo-vernacular and other 'traditional' styles in new development. In some places local planning authorities reacted to these trends by identifying neighbourhoods where 'character' was to be maintained. As such, they were distinguished both from conservation areas and those areas generally allocated for residential use. Apparently a 'half-way house' category. Until recently, the indications had been that such a procedure was rare. Hendry[3] had maintained that there was generally little support for them in Britain. Gould[4] had reported that they had been supported by inspectors considering appeals against refusals of planning consent, but had been seen as socially divisive by some Labour-controlled councils on the grounds that they appeared to be distinguishing favoured from less favoured areas (as do conservation areas). Their use had been rejected in Richmond-upon-Thames in favour of reliance on strong authority-wide policies, as explained later in this chapter. Nevertheless, their use was found to be unexpectedly widespread. The 1993 RTPI Conservation study had found that 23 per cent of nearly 200 local planning authorities surveyed had claimed to use them. They tended to be clustered in the large conurbations and the south of England. In an appendix to the RTPI study, Hendry[5] now described how they had come to Belfast.

The author's own investigations found that a significant number of planning authorities in London and the South-east England had adopted them independently as a defence against 'town cramming'. This had been done without reference to any guidance from theory or practice, for it does not exist. Their inventors had encountered a significant problem, that of defining the character to be conserved and they had responded with varying degrees of success. Their responses required, in effect, a consideration of criteria for implicit, sometimes explicit, objectives. This led on, in some instances, to the provision of advisory material. Control procedures were also described, often in detail, as this was the planning officers' perspective, if not that of the public.

As has been said, more cases were found than had been expected or that could be included in this chapter. In order to review their development in a convenient manner two geographical groupings were selected: **outer London** and the **Chiltern Hills**. Again, apologies are offered to those authorities whose work has not been described.

Outer London Boroughs

Occupying a ring between approximately 7 and 14 miles from central London and consisting predominantly of low- and medium-density suburbs, the outer Boroughs of Greater London have faced pressure for redevelopment at higher densities for several decades. Consequently they have been presented with the question of how much, and to what degree, the character of their suburban environment should be conserved. A significant number of outer London authorities have made use of areas of special residential character. The experiences of two of the pioneers, Redbridge and Sutton, are described below together with the contrasting position of Richmond-upon-Thames which, notwithstanding innovative work in the past, has turned its back on special areas in favour of a uniformly high level of control.

The outer London Boroughs were formed in 1964 from smaller authorities by a reorganization that created a two-tier structure. The Greater London Council (GLC), as the upper tier, was responsible for strategic planning and the London Boroughs, as the lower tier, were responsible for local planning. Prior to the formation of the GLC the authorities from which most of the outer Boroughs were formed were subject to local County Councils for planning purposes. Their

policies formed the basis of the GLC's Initial Development Plan (IDP) of 1971. This was superseded by the GLC's first and only structure plan, the Greater London Development Plan (GLDP) in 1976. The GLC was abolished in 1985 and the London Boroughs became unitary authorities exercising most, but not all, local government functions. They were required to produce Unitary Development Plans (UDPs) within guidance issued by the Department of the Environment.[6] Policies in the previous local plans (where they existed) could be carried through into the UDPs. Guidance was also provided by the London Planning Advisory Commission (LPAC).[7]

The Chiltern Hills area

The Chiltern Hills lie 20–30 miles north-west of London astride the outer edge of the Metropolitan Green Belt. This attractive area has been designated an Area of Outstanding Natural Beauty (AONB). Unfortunately, its very attractiveness coupled with its accessibility from London by road and rail, has made it a very desirable place to live. The residents have, not unexpectedly, become concerned about 'town cramming' whereby pressure for new development was relieved by building within the boundaries of existing towns rather than encroaching on the open countryside. This part of the country has, therefore, been fertile ground for the growth of proposals for conserving the character of existing residential areas.

As in outer London, a number of planning authorities in this area were found to be using residential character areas. The examples of Chiltern and Wycombe District Councils are described below together with the proposals of Dacorum Borough Council which has fully adopted the design area approach. Chiltern and Wycombe Districts are part of Buckinghamshire and are subject to its County Structure Plan.[8] Dacorum is in Hertfordshire and subject to its Structure Plan.[9]

The Redbridge Residential Precincts

The London Borough of Redbridge occupies a swathe of suburbia in the north-east of greater London which

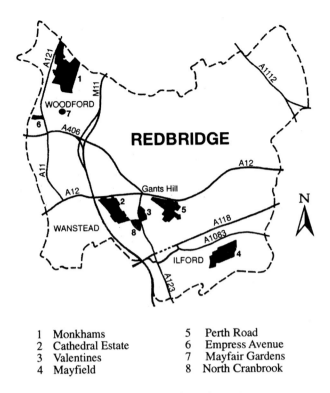

1 Monkhams   5 Perth Road
2 Cathedral Estate   6 Empress Avenue
3 Valentines   7 Mayfair Gardens
4 Mayfield   8 North Cranbrook

Figure 5.2 The Redbridge Residential Precincts

crosses the boundary between the extensive residential developments of the late nineteenth century and the villas and semi-detached houses from the 1930s. It contains a diverse range of local communities and economic fortunes. The Redbridge Residential Precincts were a significant attempt to identify small residential areas that possessed features worthy of conservation but which would not have been thought to be of sufficient historic or architectural merit to be worthy of **conservation area** status. They enjoyed strong support from residents expressed through the political process. In 1991 the Borough decided to incorporate the precincts into its new Unitary Development Plan and this process gave rise to controversies that highlighted many of the arguments put forward in this book.

The first residential precinct was designated by resolution of the Council in 1970. The first Council minute on the subject dated from 1969 and the idea appears to have originated in the concerns of the residents. Between 1970 and 1994 eight precincts were designated. Their locations are shown by Figure 5.2. An explanatory leaflet was produced for each

precinct and part of that for the Monkhams precinct is illustrated by Figure 5.3 as an example. At the time, the concept appears to have been unique to Redbridge and did not draw upon any published planning methodology, government guidance or explicit provision in legislation that was in existence at the time. It was also significant that there was no up-to-date local development plan in operation between 1969 and 1994, an example of the general complaint made in Chapter 2. The 1957 County Development Plan for Metropolitan Essex[10] had been adopted by the Borough in 1965. A town centre plan for Ilford had been adopted in 1980 but it did not incorporate any of the residential precincts. No comprehensive local plan for the Borough existed until the Unitary Development Plan was adopted in 1994.[11]

Throughout the 'plan-less' period the residential precincts appeared to have support not only from the residents but also from the Department of the Environment inspectors called upon to determine appeals against refusal of planning consent. Officers were of the opinion that the proportion of refusals and appeals was lower in the precincts than other residential parts of the Borough.

My overall impression is that the residential precinct policy has the effect of raising the standard of submissions because it leads to a greater awareness among applicants to achieve a high quality of design. Where this is not the case the residential precinct policy certainly helps us in our negotiations with applicants to achieve improvements in design. Whilst the policy itself is rarely a direct reason for refusal, it is used to support a refusal on the grounds of poor design or being out of character with the area concerned. I believe that this approach has been successful in Monkhams Residential Precinct in particular, where the quality of applications is generally quite high and in what used to be Mayfield Residential Precinct which was also generally successful in achieving high quality developments prior to designation as a Conservation Area. I believe the policy was supported on appeal; not so much as a direct reason for dismissal but in terms of recognizing the special character of the area concerned.[12]

Although the precincts were adopted by resolution of the Council, apparently no detailed criteria for their designation were approved. Some latent or implicit criteria must have been used on occasions. One precinct emerged only after being refused conservation area status and at least two areas had requests by local

Policy Statement.

Social and Physical Identity

Monkhams, a well defined area (about 200 acres) of predominantly residential character, is bounded by the Central Line to the east; the Borough boundary and Epping Forest to the north; The Green, Inmans Row, Barclay Oval, Aldeburgh Place and High Road, Woodford Green to the west; and Harts Hospital and the rear boundaries of houses fronting Monkhams Avenue to the south.

The boundaries have no statutory significance, but identify a community with its own special character.

Development Plan Provisions

The estate is reserved for primarily residential purposes in the Initial Development Plan. It was almost fully developed during the inter-war period (1919-1939) by the erection of single family houses on large plots with generous spaces between buildings.

There are no major highway or planning proposals likely to affect the area. However, in response to economic pressures the character of the area could undergo radical change because of piecemeal redevelopment of large plots and conversions of individual houses into two or more flats

Policy Criteria:

(i)   No non-residential uses should normally be permitted which would alter its residential character. Whilst this does not preclude some educational and institutional uses, these are to be associated with residential occupation.

Suburban Character

New building as well as works of restoration and improvement are bound to involve changes, but these should take place without detracting from the character of the area. Although its architecture is not outstanding its distinction lies quite simply in the architectural unity and its contrasting greenery. This unity would be lost if the existing did not influence the design of new development. It is important to distinguish between restoration and new work; the former should respect the integrity of the style of architecture and reflect its craftsmanship and appearance, whilst the new work should take full advantage of modern technology.

Policy Criteria:

(ii)   New work in scale, form and materials should be in sympathy with existing development and should not obtrude, especially on prominent sites. New development should be well-designed for function and appearance; the overall form and component parts of elevations should have satisfactory proportions.

Density

The boundary contains approximately 1,400 dwellings. The average density of development is approximately 68 persons per hectare (28 p.p.a.) and 100 habitable rooms per hectare (41 h.r.a.). The occupancy rate is about 0.68 persons per habitable room.

Policy Criteria:

(iii)   New development proposals should be in scale with the area and at a density not exceeding 125 habitable rooms per hectare (50 h.r.a.). Conversions of existing dwellings into flats or maisonettes should not normally be permitted, particularly where they result in loss of privacy or accommodation below Parker Morris standards.

(iv)   New development should comply with reasonable daylighting and sunlighting standards as it affects the site of the proposal and the surrounding land.

Redevelopment

The dwellings are mostly two-storey detached and semi-detached houses built largely between 1919 and 1939. Some dwellings mainly in the southern part of the precinct and on the High Road, Woodford Green frontage were built before 1914 but are generally in first class condition. Nevertheless, it is amongst this latter group, where one dwelling often occupies a comparatively large site, that there is likely to be pressure for renewal or redevelopment.

Redevelopment normally takes place at a higher density with its consequent loss of gardens and the visual detraction of hard-standings and ungaraged vehicles. Whilst recognising the need for smaller dwelling units, appropriate and economic redevelopment should protect the existing amenities whilst preventing obsolescence, multiple occupation and neglect.

Policy Criteria:

(v)   The continuous cycle of renewal and redevelopment prompted by the economic use of land should enhance and not depress environmental standards. There should be adequate amenity in terms of garden space, terraces or private balconies.

(vi)   Flats should not normally be permitted unless there are exceptional circumstances.

Figure 5.3 The Monkhams Residential Precinct. Extract from the leaflet produced by the LB of Redbridge

Environmental Standards

Monkhams is fortunate in its spaciousness and in its freedom from industrial and commercial intrusions. The local shopping centre is attractive, compact and conveniently located for the estate and for public transport.

Policy Criteria:

(vii) The precinct should be protected from intrusion by traffic noise and also from extraneous traffic. Proposals for garaging and parking should be unobtrusive. Garages or car ports projecting in front of building lines should not normally be permitted.

(viii) Exceptionally it may be appropriate to close roads so that they become culs-de-sac or allow for the provision of safe pedestrian crossings.

Planting and Open Space

The environment is here greatly enhanced by both private and public gardens, whilst mature groups of trees amongst the houses and in the adjoining recreation ground provide a link with the Forest which seems never to be far away.

Policy Criteria:

(ix) New buildings should be sited with the object of preserving as many of the existing trees as possible. All submitted plans should include surveys of all trees and shrubs on the sites together with adequate landscaping proposals. New planting may be required particularly where any loss is caused. The existing areas of amenity open space should be maintained and improved. The finer trees need to be protected by Tree Preservation Orders.

FOR FURTHER INFORMATION: Contact the Borough Planning & Development Officer at the Town Hall, High Road, Ilford, or telephone (01)-478 3020 Extension 356.

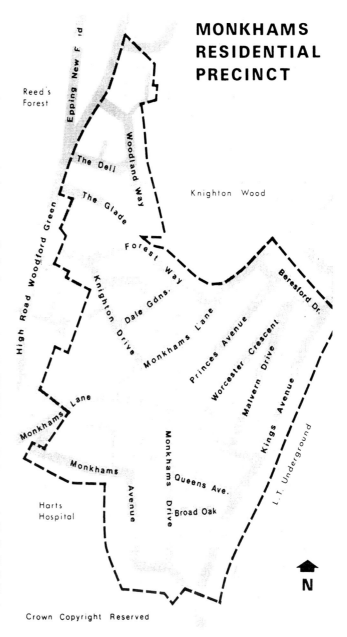

Crown Copyright Reserved

Figure 5.3 (continued) The Monkhams Residential Precinct. Extract from the leaflet produced by the LB of Redbridge

residents for precinct status turned down. Following one such rejection, a definition by the Chairman of the Planning Committee was minuted as follows:

The Chairman replied that a residential precinct was a residential area of a character of its own. This character could derive either from the architectural layout or the landscaping or combination of these.[13]

The explanatory leaflets contained a description of the character of each area in general terms, as would be acceptable to a lay readership, and set out the policy of the Council for that precinct under the headings of land-use, density, redevelopment, design, and environmental standards.

Problems and disputes began to arise when it came to the incorporation of the residential precincts into the draft Unitary Development Plan (UDP). Prior to this stage the leaflets had had the status of supplementary planning guidance and did not form part of any statutory development plan, although this had not, apparently prevented them from functioning effectively. The proposed plan contained general policies that affected urban design in residential areas:

- residential land was not, normally, to be converted to other uses;
- a minimum density was specified for new housing development;
- the scope for the conversion of existing dwellings into smaller units was restricted;
- the Council would take into account neighbourliness, design, materials, appearance, suitability for use, sunlight and general relationship to surroundings for all new development, including extensions.

There followed a section on conservation areas and one on the residential precincts, all of which were identified on the Proposals Map. The residential precinct policies went into more detail than the conservation area policies, quoting a maximum residential density and making special comments on the Monkhams, Mayfield and Valentines precincts.

This section of the UDP received 150 objections. One, from a house builder, argued that the definition of the precinct concept was imprecise. The majority of the 150 argued that it should be applied to all residential areas in the Borough. From the point of view of

the objectors, the concept should have been either extended or abandoned. In his report on the public inquiry into the objections to the UDP the inspector came down in favour of abandonment, recommending deletion of the residential precincts from the plan on the following grounds:

- it was difficult to understand the application of the criteria;
- some precincts had policies that were more restrictive than those applying in the conservation areas;
- the general policies on housing and design would protect all residential areas.

The Borough officers disagreed with this recommendation and received strong support from councillors. A reworded version of the policy was included in the Council's modifications to the deposit version of the plan and, ultimately, in the adopted UDP.

To what extent did the Redbridge Residential Precincts anticipate the proposals made here? There were similarities to the concept of the **design area** but no attempt was made to apply them to all residential areas and they were used only when the objective was one of conservation. Apart from the implicit objective of a high degree of conservation no explicit statements of objectives were made. General descriptions of character were provided but nothing that could be seen as an exact definition. The policies stated could be seen as attempts at what are called **criteria** in Chapters 3 and 4. The most significant absence, when compared to the proposals in Chapter 3, was that of the **advisory material**. No examples were approved for the residents or their agents to follow.

Nothing in the paragraph above, or in this book as a whole should be taken as representing especial criticism of Redbridge. On the contrary the Borough is to be congratulated on its initiatives and they are described here because they go much further than those of most other planning authorities. On the other hand, it is difficult not to have some sympathy with the critics of the logical basis of the Borough's initiatives. It is difficult to perceive the differences in intention between a **precinct** and a **conservation area**. The implication contained in the committee minutes and discussions with officers was that the conservation area was seen as a strong concept, appropriate to very high quality and historic environments, but differing from the precincts only in degree. This interpretation anticipates one of the principal arguments of this book, that level of intervention be made explicit. However, this is not really a straightforward interpretation in the Redbridge context. As the inspector for the local plan inquiry commented, some precincts appeared to have stricter controls than those in conservation areas and others had policies that were indistinguishable from those in the conservation areas. As some objectors commented, the criteria for identifying desirable character were not made clear when, for example, some residents had wanted their area designated as a precinct but were turned down. Moreover, a conservation area designation in its legal essentials provided only the power to prevent demolition.[14] Why then were not all the precincts made conservation areas?

The problem would appear to lie in the confusion between means and ends identified in Chapters 1 and 2. There is a difference between the objective to conserve and the legal device of conservation area designation which is a control procedure of limited scope. Where the precincts have been a good idea has been in making clear **what** was being conserved. They were in essence a way of stating design objectives. However, there has been confusion among all parties about the various means available. If general demolition control had always existed in the standard British planning legislation then conservation areas as a control procedure should not be necessary. As it stands, and given that it is comparatively easy to designate a conservation area (almost as easy as designating a residential precinct), perhaps all the precincts should have been so designated creating a situation similar to that in Richmond (see section below). If the Borough felt that differing degrees of or qualities of conservation were appropriate then this could have been made clear by stating different objectives. Nevertheless, the Redbridge precincts represented a significant step forward.

London Borough of Sutton

The London Borough of Sutton lies in the south-west part of Greater London. It was formed from the older local government units of Sutton, Carshalton and Wallington and consists predominantly of areas of inter-war housing, some being large council estates, some areas of large expensive houses, and the rest of middle-income private housing. There are some small

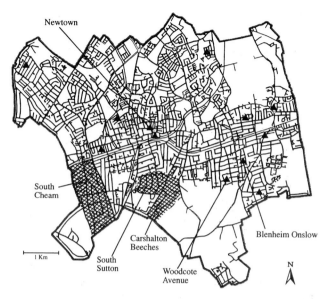

▲ Areas of Special Local Character

Figure 5.4 LB of Sutton: location of Conservation Areas, Areas of Special Local Character and Special Areas. © Crown copyright

areas of historic interest but they do not approach the scale of those in Richmond and, similarly, the nineteenth-century portions do not approach the scale of those in Redbridge. Nevertheless, Sutton has one of the longest histories of the promotion of special residential areas and, after Richmond, one of the strongest positions on the control of residential design.

In the late 1960s, the Borough identified three 'higher density areas', ranging in size from 65 to 115 hectares, where redevelopment at a higher density was to be encouraged. Success was variable and by the late 1970s only 17 per cent of the aggregate area had been so developed. General design control in this period was limited to the application of quantitative standards but, nevertheless, two further areas were identified where further controls to maintain their landscape dominated suburban character were considered appropriate, mainly as a result of pressure from residents. They were South Cheam, in 1971, and Carshalton Beeches, in 1974. Their locations are shown in Figure 5.4. Control was exercised over plot size, building lines, building materials and, in Carshalton Beeches, dwellings were restricted to two-storey houses with pitched roofs. The objective was maintenance of heavily landscaped low-density suburban form rather than townscape quality.

During the 1970s thinking moved away from redevelopment at higher densities and towards conservation and refurbishment. Eight 'areas of special local character' were identified where the enhancement of older residential fabric would be encouraged. In 1978 a report[15] was published in preparation for a new District Plan.[16] It reviewed the policy on design control and concluded that more general guidance was necessary as quantitative standards did not ensure quality of urban design. The resulting 1981 District Plan abandoned the higher density areas, confirmed the special policies for Carshalton Beeches and South Cheam and designated the eight areas of special local character. During the early and mid-1980s, additional special areas claimed the attention of planning officers and informal policy statements were produced. The low-density environment of South Sutton took on the same restrictive regime as South Cheam and Carshalton Beeches. Three more areas of special local character

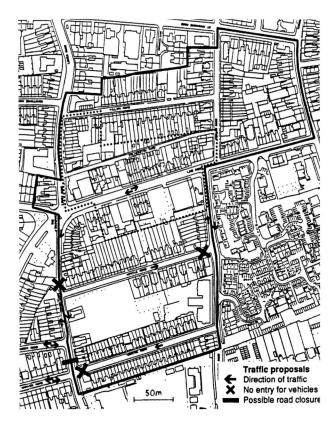

Traffic proposals
← Direction of traffic
✗ No entry for vehicles
▬ Possible road closure

50m

Figure 5.5 Map of the Newtown Special Area, LB of Sutton. © Crown copyright

were identified but this time they were higher quality areas, to be conserved rather than enhanced.

The most interesting innovation was the production of informal policies for a mixed area of residential and employment uses called Newtown. Its location is shown in Figure 5.4 and its plan in Figure 5.5. This area had been intended for redevelopment as light industry and the residents had become distressed at the difficulty in mortgaging their houses. A new policy of conservation and mixed uses was introduced. These additions proved popular and, in the case of Newtown, achieved much practical success regarding mortgage lending. Both the additional and original areas were incorporated into the 1988 local plan.[17] This policy was carried through into the 1994 Unitary Development Plan[18] which, in addition to the 11 existing areas, suggested that two more might be identified by the Council. The Council also committed itself to preparing detailed guidance for all the areas at a later date as such guidance was given in the Plan for only three of them. No problems were encountered at the local plan inquiry with any of these special area policies because the policies were being brought forward from an existing statutory development plan.

The proposals for the special areas were additional to the general design policies applying to all development in the UDP. Most importantly:

E51: Proposals shall be of a high standard of design and layout, integrating all components of a development from the outset.

E52: Development shall be compatible with existing townscape in terms of mass, impact and height and shall avoid sharp contrasts of scale, building form, style and landscape.

E53: Development proposals shall make suitable provision for hard and soft landscape. . . Such landscape shall afford screening and privacy for the proposed development and shall contribute to the promotion of a satisfactory townscape. (Sections 4.122–4.128)

Residential development was subject to the following additional policies:

- permitted only if existing amenities, character, appearance and ecological value were not affected;
- suitable frontage infill was favoured;
- loss of back garden land of ecological value was opposed;

- proposals out of character with the surrounding residential environment were opposed;
- corner site development would be favourably considered

In implementing the above policies the Council intended that all development should take account of its design guidance provided in the Plan. This contained much advisory information on shopfronts, advertisements, house extensions, house conversions, corner sites, front garden parking, new streets, residential parking areas and residential layout. At times, principles very similar to those in the Essex Guide were described.

By implication, these general policies and the design guidance were not considered sufficient in themselves to conserve the character of the special areas. The UDP spelled out further detailed guidance for the special policy areas and three of the areas of 'special local character', Newtown, Woodcote and Blenheim-Onslow. Plans of these last three areas are shown in Figures 5.5–5.7. Policies for the remaining special areas were to be published at a later date.

Special Policy Areas

The following were specified for Carshalton Beeches:

- minimum plot dimensions;
- distance of building line from frontages;
- back-to-back spacing;
- detached two-storey houses;
- pitched roofs;
- landscaping schemes retaining existing trees;
- space for two cars, plus caravan or boat, behind the building line.

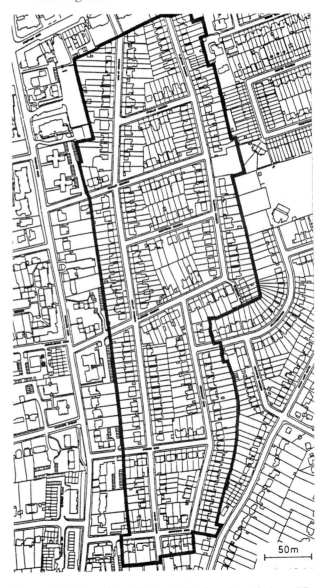

Figure 5.6 Map of the Woodcote Special Area, LB of Sutton. © Crown copyright

Figure 5.7 Map of the Blenheim/Onslow Special Area, LB of Sutton. © Crown copyright

Specification for South Sutton was the same apart from the fact that parking (including the boat) was permitted in front of the building line. South Cheam was the same except that infill in the form of culs-de-sac or squares, not connecting with main roads, was permitted for plots with depths greater than 107 m.

Newton area of special local character

Detailed procedures on mixed uses, directed towards improvement of the area, were set out. The area had previous industrial use but no character analysis was provided. No advisory information on redevelopment was given.

Woodcote Avenue area of special local character

The policy statement set out what amounted to a description of the objectives and control procedures, albeit very briefly, under the headings of land-use, intensity of development, building form, back-land development, parking, landscape, and nature conservation. No advisory information was provided.

Blenheim/Onslow area of special local character

This policy statement contained a good general description of the area which identified the salient features of its character. As with the Woodcote Avenue area, a large number of headings were used but the specification of form and style went somewhat further. It is of significant interest and is reproduced as Figure 5.8. Policy BLE3 represented the **objective** for which the specification is the **criteria**.

The question is, as with the other examples, to what extent did these areas approximate to the design areas proposed in Chapter 3? The edges were correctly drawn along back-garden boundaries for the Woodcote and Blenheim/Onslow areas as can be seen from Figures 5.6 and 5.7, but for the areas of intensity control some of the edges were drawn along roads. For the Newton area all the edges were along the centre lines of roads as can be seen from Figure 5.5. The statements for the areas of intensity control were strong on criteria for fulfilment of objectives but little else. Moreover, the objectives themselves were not specified. Those for the

POLICY BLE3

ANY NEW RESIDENTIAL DEVELOPMENT SHALL RESPECT THE GENERAL FORM OF THE OLDER PROPERTIES IN THE AREA AND SHALL CONFORM TO THE CRITERIA SET OUT IN THIS STATEMENT

5.5 In cases where it is not clear how this policy should be applied, the older properties are those which were constructed before 1920. The following criteria are set out for the guidance of developers in accordance with Policy BLE3. In assessing applications for new development, the Local Planning Authority will judge whether the designs sufficiently satisfy the intentions of the policy.

Plot Sizes And Densities

6.1 Although 175 square metres is considered to be the minimum amount of land required for the satisfactory provision of a family house where a development site straddles the Area boundary, this must be regarded as a rare exception. To assist retaining the existing pattern of development elsewhere in the Area:

POLICY BLE4

REDEVELOPMENT WILL BE EXPECTED TO BE CONFINED WITHIN EXISTING PLOT BOUNDARIES

6.2 The recommendations concerning the 'footprints' of buildings which are written into paragraph 5.27 of the UDP. In this area, it is suggested that, unless a Planning Brief applies, not more, than two existing plots should be amalgamated to form one redevelopment site. This would, for example, enable the construction of a pair of semi-detached houses or a small block of flats.

Respect For Existing Form

7.1 In furtherance of the aims of Policy BLE3, designs for new development should also ensure that:

- the highest point or line of the roof of any new building in the Area is not substantially higher or lower than that of the neighbouring buildings, excluding any which are outside the Area boundary;
- any new building, including flats, is provided with a pitched roof. Mansard roofs, which are foreign to the architecture of the Area, will be unacceptable;
- no new building exceeds three storeys including any storey in the roof;
- where proposed, in a new building, dormer windows are provided with pitched roofs; and
- the appearance of all new buildings, including flats, should resemble, as far possible, detached or semi-detached single detached dwellings and should have similar 'footprints'.

7.2 The requirements in relation to dormer windows, are commended to householders who may be contemplating loft conversions as is also the use of roof lights. Such windows would be more in keeping with the established architectural features of the Area.

Respect For The Older Styles

8.1 Except at significantly higher cost, the construction techniques and style of the pre-1920 buildings cannot be exactly replicated on redevelopment. In practical terms, the best that can be achieved is a pastiche, within a modern context, of the older designs and decorations in the Area.

8.2 In seeking to achieve the aims of Policy BLE3, certain elements of the older architecture should be present in plans submitted for planning approval. The following list, which is not meant to be exhaustive, is commended to potential developers: Dark red or, occasionally, London Stock bricks, Grey slate or plain dark red tiles; Gabled bays; Older window sizes with transoms to match original sash designs; Decorative brick or stonework; White or pale render and black mock timbering; Canopies and porches.

Figure 5.8 Extract from the Policies for the Blenheim/Onslow Special Area, LB of Sutton UDP Deposit Draft 1994

Woodcote Avenue and Blenheim/Onslow areas were much stronger on objectives and character description.

Statements for all areas were weak on the provision of advisory information. It was possible to discern a movement towards a more objective-driven approach over time. The areas for which policies were first devised had edges drawn along roads and policies specified in the form of standards. Character analysis, objectives and boundaries along backs of properties came with the later areas.

What was significant about the Sutton experience was that, even though there had been extensive local

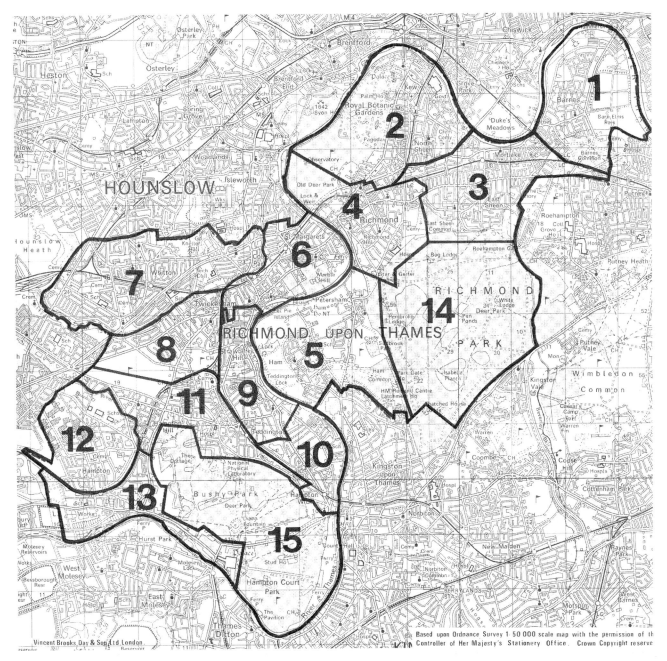

Figure 5.9 Sub-areas from the 1981 Environmental Character Study, LB of Richmond-upon-Thames. © Crown copyright

plan coverage with evolving design policies over a considerable period, it was still found necessary to establish residential character zones. Within these zones there was, in turn, a gradual increase in the degree of detail provided as the need to specify character was confronted.

London Borough of Richmond-upon-Thames

One of the most significant British planning authorities for guidance on design and conservation is the London Borough of Richmond-upon-Thames. The

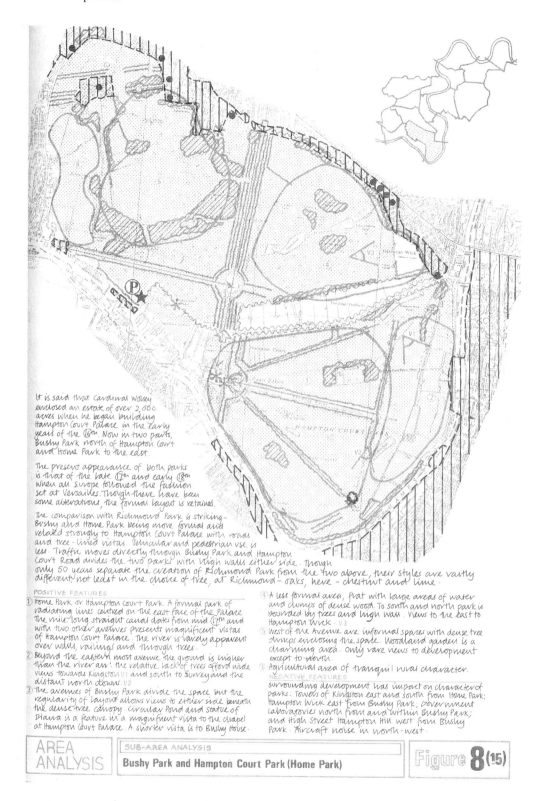

It is said that Cardinal Wolsey enclosed an estate of over 2,000 acres when he began building Hampton Court Palace in the early years of the 16th. Now in two parts, Bushy Park north of Hampton Court and Home Park to the east.

The present appearance of both parks is that of the late 17th and early 18th when all Europe followed the fashion set at Versailles. Though there have been some alterations, the formal layout is retained.

The comparison with Richmond Park is striking - Bushy and Home Park being more formal and related strongly to Hampton Court Palace with roads and tree-lined vistas. Vehicular and pedestrian use is less. Traffic moves directly through Bushy Park and Hampton Court Road divides the two parks with high walls either side. Though only 50 years separate the creation of Richmond Park from the two above, their styles are vastly different, not least in the choice of tree, at Richmond - oaks, here - chestnut and lime.

POSITIVE FEATURES

1. Home Park or Hampton Court Park. A formal park of radiating lines centred on the east face of the Palace. The mile long straight canal dates from mid 17th and with two other avenues present magnificent vistas of Hampton Court Palace. The river is rarely apparent over walls, railings and through trees.
2. Beyond the eastern most avenue the ground is higher than the river arm: the relative lack of trees afford wide views towards Kingston V1 and south to Surrey and the distant north downs. V2
3. The avenues of Bushy Park divide the space but the regularity of layout allows views to either side beneath the dense tree canopy. Circular Pond and statue of Diana is a feature in a magnificent vista to the chapel at Hampton Court Palace. A shorter vista is to Bushy House.

4. A less formal area, flat with large areas of water and clumps of dense wood. To south and north park is bounded by trees and high wall. Views to the east to Hampton Wick. V3
5. West of the Avenue are informal spaces with dense tree clumps enclosing the space. Woodland garden is a charming area. Only rare views to development except to north.
6. Agricultural area of tranquil rural character.

NEGATIVE FEATURES

Surrounding development has impact on character of parks. Towers of Kingston east and south from Home Park; Hampton Wick east from Bushy Park; Government laboratories north from and within Bushy Park; and High Street Hampton Hill west from Bushy Park. Aircraft noise in north-west.

AREA ANALYSIS

SUB-AREA ANALYSIS

Bushy Park and Hampton Court Park (Home Park)

Figure 8 (15)

Figure 5.10 Sub-area analysis for Barnes from the 1981 Environmental Character Study, LB of Richmond

Borough occupies a wedge of territory in the south-west of Greater London containing much middle- to high-income suburbia and, more importantly, several royal parks, palaces and a large number of other outstanding historic buildings and townscapes. It was originally two separate local government units, Richmond and Twickenham, lying on opposite banks of the Thames.

In 1981 a study was prepared which was of exceptional quality and of great relevance to the arguments put forward here. This was the *Environmental Character*[19] report published as preparatory work for the 1985 *District Plan*.[20]

What was innovatory was the next step by which the Borough was divided into 15 'sub-areas' as shown in Figure 5.9. These were larger than the design areas proposed here and were not derived explicitly from design objectives. Nevertheless, they covered the whole of the planning authority's area, not just the historic and other high quality parts. The positive and negative characteristics were analysed in some detail as illustrated by the example in Figure 5.10. Among the categories used for analysis, listed in Figure 5.11 were 'inappropriate permitted development', 'areas where change would be desirable', possibilities for tree planting and 'possibilities for improvement'. Although all the categories were, to some extent, subjective and implied the existence of aesthetic objectives, they also carried the implication of action in pursuit of policy, and for all parts of the Borough. It was disappointing to find that neither the River Thames and its environs nor any of the major roads or parks were made separate sub-areas. The river and its environs was, nevertheless, analysed as a 'special area' in Chapter 4 of the report and it was further subdivided and analysed by these subdivisions in an appendix.

Another important and innovative feature was the report's development and analysis of 'residential development categories':

A classification of residential area by age of construction is useful in distinguishing architectural styles and in dealing with detail design. However, the Council as Local Planning Authority is also concerned with the overall environment of the area, in which case a classification that concentrates upon the space between buildings, their height, size of front gardens, vegetation and the relationship between height of buildings and the width of the street is more appropriate. These aspects can be linked into the categories set out below.

Important areas of trees and woodland
Important avenues of trees
Open areas
Outstanding areas of townscape
Views
Vistas
Concentrations of historic buildings
Visual entry points to parks
Walls or buildings that form strong visual edge to development
Attractive residential areas
Landmarks
Heavy traffic
Parking clutter
Forecourt parking
Advertisement clutter
Development out of character or scale with surroundings
Possibilities for tree planting
Possibilities for improvement
Areas where development has a significant impact on major open areas
Areas where change would be desirable
Industry/commerce detrimental to surroundings
Inappropriate permitted development

Figure 5.11 Key to sub-area analysis maps from the 1981 Environmental Character Study, LB of Richmond

1. Dispersed, informal environment of large detached houses in their grounds with dense vegetation and winding streets.

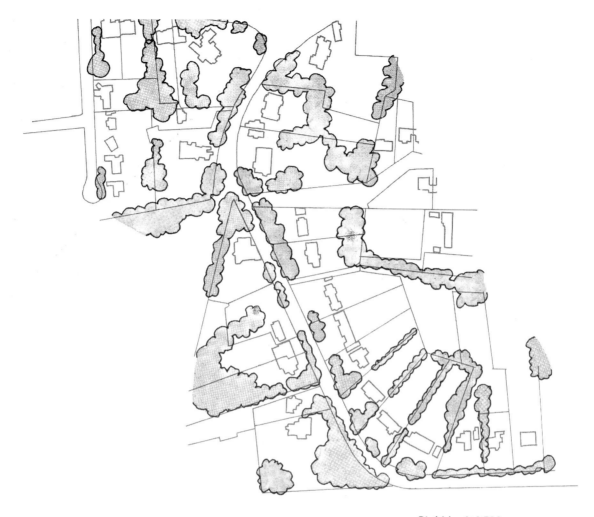

PLAN 1:2500

SECTION 1:2500

Space between buildings: 30-40m   Front gardens: 10-20m   Back gardens: up to 60m+

- Low density 2 storey detached houses in large gardens.
- Informal layout of roads and buildings.
- Long front gardens with dense vegetation.
- Trees and shrubs often obscure views of houses.

PROBLEMS

- Areas are stable and unchanging. Few problems, but some pressure to develop.
- In some areas large plots are sold to be redeveloped as small estates of houses or flats.

EXAMPLES

- Relatively few areas - most having been in-filled or redeveloped.
- East Sheen - Christchurch Road/Fife Road and environs. Mostly Edwardian inter-war and post-war
- Petersham - mostly Georgian and post-war.

Figure 5.12 Extract from the Categories of Residential Environment in the 1981 Environmental Character Study, LB of Richmond

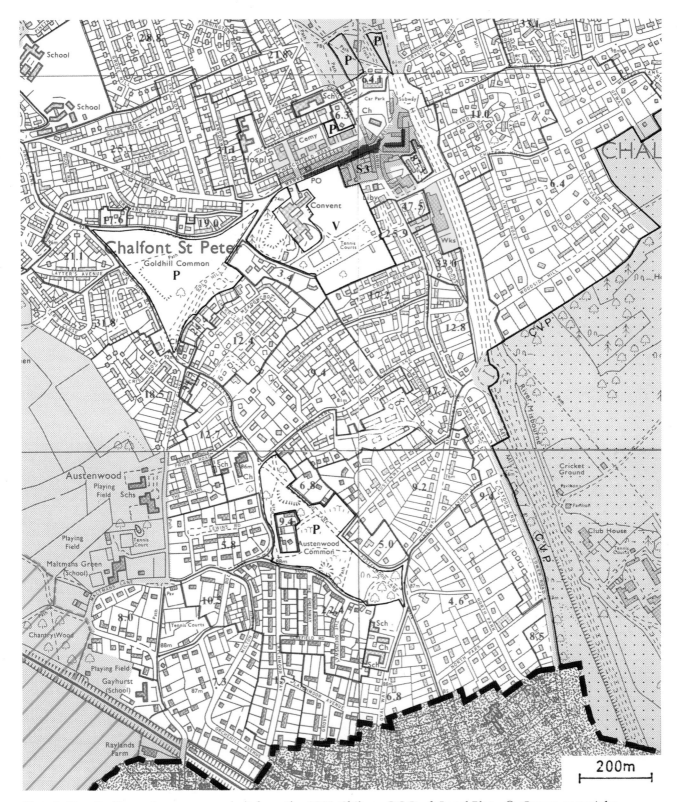

Plate 1 Density Zones (now superseded) from the 1991 Chiltern DC Draft Local Plan. © Crown copyright

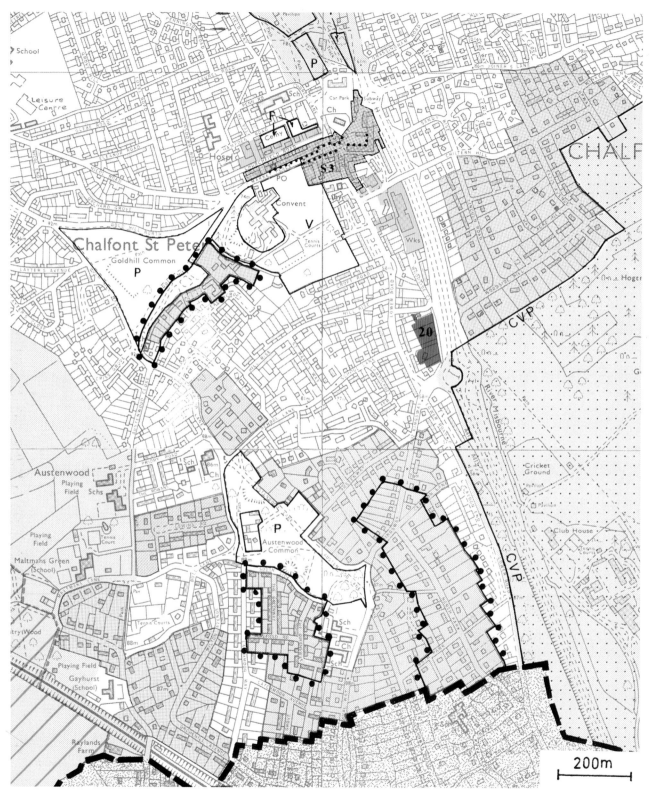

Plate 2 Special Character Zones from the 1993 Chiltern DC Draft Local Plan. © Crown copyright

RESIDENTIAL CHARACTER ZONES

RC1   Established Residential Zones

RC1+2   Special Character Zones

RC1+3   Spacious Residential Zones

RC1+5   Residential Enhancement Zones

North

200m

Plate 3   Residential Character Zones from the Wycombe District Local Plan Proposals Map.

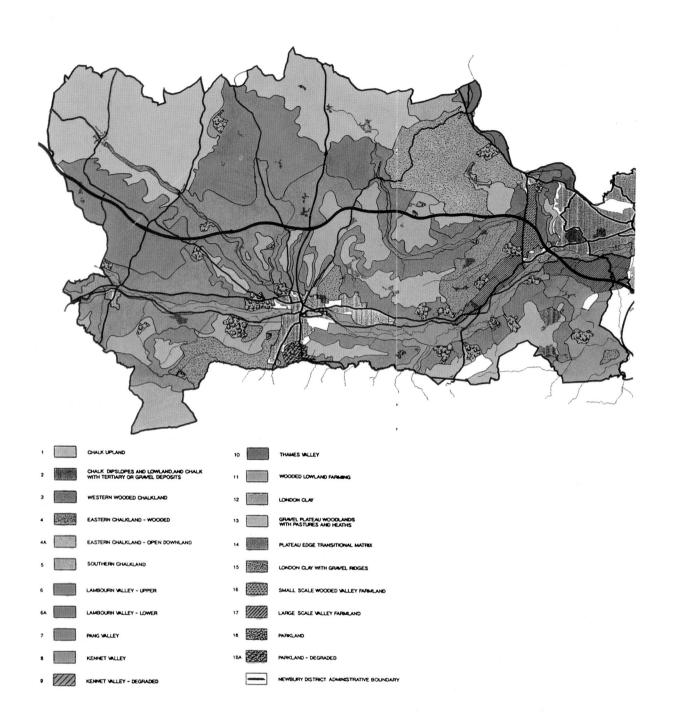

1		CHALK UPLAND	10		THAMES VALLEY
2		CHALK DIPSLOPES AND LOWLAND,AND CHALK WITH TERTIARY OR GRAVEL DEPOSITS	11		WOODED LOWLAND FARMING
3		WESTERN WOODED CHALKLAND	12		LONDON CLAY
4		EASTERN CHALKLAND - WOODED	13		GRAVEL PLATEAU WOODLANDS WITH PASTURES AND HEATHS
4A		EASTERN CHALKLAND - OPEN DOWNLAND	14		PLATEAU EDGE TRANSITIONAL MATRIX
5		SOUTHERN CHALKLAND	15		LONDON CLAY WITH GRAVEL RIDGES
6		LAMBOURN VALLEY - UPPER	16		SMALL SCALE WOODED VALLEY FARMLAND
6A		LAMBOURN VALLEY - LOWER	17		LARGE SCALE VALLEY FARMLAND
7		PANG VALLEY	18		PARKLAND
8		KENNET VALLEY	18A		PARKLAND - DEGRADED
9		KENNET VALLEY - DEGRADED			NEWBURY DISTRICT ADMINISTRATIVE BOUNDARY

Plate 4 Newbury District Council Landscape Character Areas.

2. Grand scale, formal street of 3, 4, 5 storey houses, detached and terraced, with strong linear form, spacious well landscaped streets and large front gardens.

3. Suburban housing development; 1, 2, 3 storey detached, semi-detached and terraced with front gardens.
    (a) small streets of uniform or mixed styles;
    (b) large homogeneous estates.

4. Tight-knit urban streets of uniform design, semi-detached or terraced, with strong linear form and rhythm; 2–3 storey with small front gardens or yards; narrow streets.

5. Terraces of small cottages and houses, 2-3 storeys in straight uniform street, with small yards or no front gardens.

6. Purpose built flats; over 4 storey and up to 12 storey towers in a variety of forms, in streets or set in landscaped space.

7. Modern cul-de-sac development; generally 2 storey in short terraces or semi-detached of uniform design, often informal winding streets with communal front gardens and small rear gardens; high percentage of garage accommodation. (Chapter 4, section 14, p. 13)

The analysis was impressive, as shown by the example in Figure 5.12, and can be compared directly with the exploratory diagrams described in Chapter 3. Problems were identified but not, unfortunately, explicitly linked to objectives. Although examples of the occurrence of each residential type within the Borough were named, the classification was not used explicitly for the development of policy for them. The categories appeared almost as a free-standing analysis and it was not made clear how they had influenced the rest of the report.

Unfortunately, the features described above were not incorporated into the 1985 local plan. This plan did contain a list of strong design policies, of much more detailed nature than were to be found in most development plans of the time, but they did not reveal any overall design philosophy. More significantly for the present argument, the number of 'sub-areas' was reduced from 15 to eight 'local areas' and three 'centres' which, in consequence, covered much broader areas of the Borough. Land-use objectives and 'policies' were set out for each one but they contained little relating to three-dimensional character. Three very

large 'areas of special character', historic localities inherited from the Greater London Development Plan were identified: Richmond–Kew, Hampton Court–Bushey Park and the River Thames. The Plan designated 40 small conservation areas.

The production of the 1992 Unitary Development Plan[21] resulted in a document that reinforced, rather than rewrote, the 1985 Plan. The wording of the general design policies was strengthened and made reference to the following topics:

- scale of development;
- layout and access;
- relationship to existing and proposed townscape;
- height;
- form;
- frontage;
- building materials;
- detailing.

However, as with most planning authorities, there was still no feel for an integrating design philosophy. The broad 'areas of special character' remained and were almost entirely covered by conservation areas. The number of 'local areas' had increased to nine by the inclusion of the Richmond centre. They were still very large and did not represent the same approach as the 1981 Study, nor that recommended in this book. As in the 1985 Plan, there were policies for them that incorporated many aspects of urban design but without an overall three-dimensional feel. General descriptions of the 'local areas' were available in the text of the written statement but nothing that approached the detailed character analysis of the 1981 study. A separate section on design standards and guidance which was very extensive, especially for shopfronts, was included.

The planning officers have expressed the view[22] that the general design policies in both the 1985 and 1992 plans had been very effective in controlling the appearance and layout of development. The 1981 study had contributed to the content of site briefs and evidence presented for appeals against refusal of planning consent. There had been pressure from the residents of some areas of mid-twentieth-century housing for special protection for their neighbourhood but this had been resisted in favour of a uniformly strict interpretation and application of the general design policies. The main reason given for the fact that the detailed analysis of the 1981 study was not carried through into the subsequent local plans was that the local plans were broader policy framework, rather than design, documents. There was evidence that the inclusion of detailed policies outside of conservation areas was resisted by the Department of the Environment. It could also be argued that the historic context and high-income inhabitants of the Borough would lead to levels of intervention that were high or very high rather than medium or low.

Chiltern District Council

Chiltern District contains a large section of the Chiltern Hills AONB. There are a number of small towns, some with historic centres, which have rail connections to central London and are, consequently, subject to intense development pressures. They already contain substantial areas of high-income housing and the existing residents were, not perhaps surprisingly, very resistant to redevelopment and 'town cramming'.

Until the development of local plans by the Council in the early 1990s, there had been no statutory local plan covering the area since the last development plan produced for Buckinghamshire under the provisions of the 1947 Town and Country Planning Act. The District Council had, since its creation in 1975, adopted, from time to time, statements of local planning policy. Nevertheless, without a development plan, applications for permission for the development and redevelopment of residential areas had been difficult to resist on appeal and the structure plan housing targets had been consistently over-fulfilled. To counter-act the pressure for the re-development of residential areas, the Council inserted into the deposit version of its 1990s local plans[23] a concept called the **residential density zone**. Such zones covered all land allocated for residential use and for each zone a density was specified, normally the existing density, in dwellings per hectare. For an example see Figure 5.13 (Plate 1). This procedure had certain similarities to density specification in town maps produced under the 1947 Town and Country Planning Act although this comparison was resisted by Council officers on the grounds that their zones were smaller than those current in the 1950s.

The policy was that development at a higher density than that specified would not be permitted.

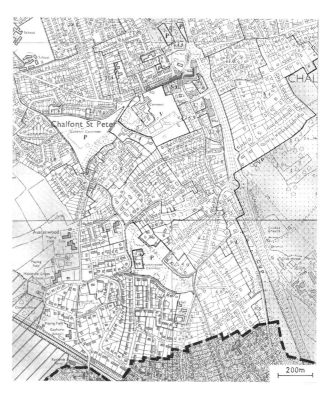

Figure 5.13 Density Zones (now superseded) from the 1991 Chiltern DC Draft Local Plan (see also Plate 1). © Crown copyright

Proposal H2 identifies 'density zones' within each of which existing residential development has broadly common characteristics in terms of dwelling type and size, curtilage size and estate layout. By requiring that the density of schemes involving the erection of new dwellings should not exceed that specified for each of the 'density zones', in relation to both the application site and the zone as a whole, the policy seeks to prevent generally the erection of new dwellings within each established residential area at densities greater than those existing in the immediate neighbourhood, in order to ensure that its character and appearance is not unduly damaged by this form of development. (para. 639 of Chesham Local Plan)

Enhanced density zones were provided where opportunities for redevelopment at a higher density were to be provided but they were small in area and comparatively few in number. They bore more resemblance to the **sites for potential development** to be found in the plans of other local authorities than to the **design areas** recommended in this study.

There were a number of objections to these proposals, mainly from developers and their agents, generally on the grounds that they were too prescriptive and did not reflect the guidance issued by central government. In his report,[24] the Inspector criticized the residential zones as too restrictive and suggested that, rather than being 'trail blazing' as the Council had claimed, they harked back to the 1932 Town and Country Planning Act. However, he liked the enhanced density zones. He recommended that the policy on residential density zones be deleted and replaced by one on **areas of special character** (in contrast to the Redbridge situation where the inspector disagreed with such a proposal when made by the local authority). The Council followed this line and, in the adopted version of the Local Plan,[25] identified a restricted number of residential areas for special protection. The result for the area illustrated in Figure 5.13 is shown in Figure 5.14 (Plate 2). In addition to the general policies in design affecting all residential areas, in the areas of special character the following features would be expected to be maintained for any new development:

- plot size;
- frontage to an existing road;
- width of frontage;
- position within plot;
- building line;
- detached/semi-detached/terrace form;
- size, design and external appearance;
- important features of street scene and landscaping;
- treatment of footways and walls.

Unfortunately, no attempt was made to specify the character of each area. 'Size design and external appearance' can cover a very wide brief as can 'important features of the street scene'. The nature of these special areas was, however, discussed in general terms in the local plan with photographs of some of them. It is worth noting that many were private estates with unadopted roads. As a result, they had not been subjected to engineers' road standards, an omission which contributes significantly to their special character and present-day appeal.

All development in the District Council area was covered by the general policy on the design of new development which is quoted in full in Figure 5.15. In addition, all residential development was subject to the following:

proposals should be compatible with the character of these areas by respecting the general density, scale, siting, height

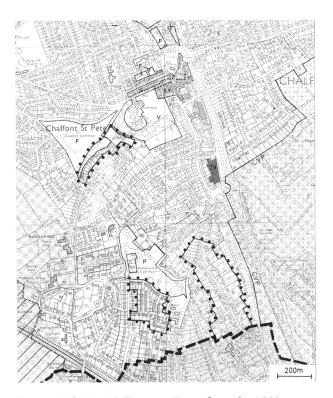

Figure 5.14 Special Character Zones from the 1993 Chiltern DC Draft Local Plan (see also Plate 2). © Crown copyright

and character of the buildings in the locality and the presence of trees, shrubs and verges. (extract from policy H2A and H2)

These policies applied both with and without density control. The interesting points were firstly, that these policies were seen as insufficient by themselves to restrain 'town cramming' and to preserve special character and, secondly, what would happen in those residential areas not subject either to density control or 'special' character designation?

Wycombe District Council

Most of the area of Wycombe District is covered by the Chilterns AONB. The district contains settlements similar to those in Chiltern District and also the medium-sized town of High Wycombe. By 1991 the Council had adopted three local plans, for High Wycombe, for the Thamesside town of Marlow and for

POLICY GC1

DESIGN OF NEW DEVELOPMENT

The Council will require a high standard of design in new buildings and extensions to existing buildings, while ensuring that it is compatible with the scale and character of surrounding development. The following detailed criteria will be taken into account:

(a) Scale of Development

The Council will generally resist any large-scale development or re-development that is considered to be out of scale and character with existing surrounding development. Account will be taken of the effect of the new development upon the natural environment, views, topography and general layout and scale of the area surrounding the application site.

(b) Layout and Access Arrangements

The layout of any new development should not be dominated by the access and parking requirements of cars and service vehicles. Large parking or servicing areas uninterrupted by landscaping will not be accepted.

(c) Scale of New Buildings

The scale of new buildings should be in harmony with the character and appearance of existing surrounding buildings, particularly with regard to frontage width and building height. Elements such as windows, doors, roofs, shop fronts etc. should relate to one another in such a way as to maintain the scale and proportions of surrounding buildings.

(d) Height of New Buildings

The height of new buildings should be in scale with the height of adjoining buildings. Where uniform building height is part of the character of a street, sharp variations in the general roof line or eaves line will not normally be permitted. In other areas, however, the continuance of irregular building heights may be acceptable where this is part of the existing character of the street scene.

(e) Form of New Buildings

The form of new buildings should reflect important features on adjoining buildings which are important to the character and appearance of the street, eg., bay windows, gable or hipped roofs and dormer windows.

(f) Siting and Relationship with Adjoining Buildings

The siting of new buildings should take into account the siting of existing adjoining buildings and the scale and alignment of the road in which they are to be located. In most cases this will mean building on the same line as existing adjoining buildings. Substantial departures from the existing alignment of buildings will only be permitted in exceptional circumstances. It may, however, in certain circumstances, be appropriate for extensions to existing buildings to be set back behind the main building line.

(g) Building Materials

In areas where certain facing materials predominate, such as the colour of bricks, or slated or clay-tiled roofs, new development should use matching or similar materials. Where an existing building is to be extended the proposed facing materials should match as closely as possible those of the original building.

(h) Detailing of Building Work

The success of a new building, or extension to an existing building, in its setting may depend on such design details as small projections, ornamentation, the use of special brickwork, the linking of particular features on adjoining buildings or the continuation of walls and fences. The consideration of such matters should therefore be given special attention at the design stage.

Figure 5.15 Design policies from the 1993 Chiltern DC Local Plan

the remaining rural areas of the District. These have since been superseded by a Districtwide local plan[26] which was adopted in 1995.

In so doing, the Council attempted to iprove its control over the design of development, especially for the residential environment. For the *Wycombe District Local Plan*, it developed five types of residential character zone.

Established residential zones

These applied to all urban residential areas. They could be overlain by other types of zone although they would apply for the majority of areas. New development had to respect the existing scale, massing, density, gardens, spaces between buildings, amenity space and density.

RESIDENTIAL CHARACTER ZONES

	RC1	Established Residential Zones
	RC1+2	Special Character Zones
	RC1+3	Spacious Residential Zones
	RC1+5	Residential Enhancement Zones

North
200m

Figure 5.16 Residential Character Zones from the Wycombe District Local Plan Proposals Map (see also Plate 3)

Special residential character zones

These were residential areas that had retained a cohesive identity. Many were conservation areas. New development had to respect the historic pattern of development of the area and, in addition to the requirements for established residential zones, was required to incorporate those aspects of materials, roofscape, building details and such other incidental features that contributed to the character of the area.

Spacious residential zones

These were areas of comparatively low density which were dominated by landscaping with mature vegetation, corresponding to the arcadian form described in Chapter 3. In addition to the requirements for established residential zones, any new development had to retain the mature landscape and generous space between buildings.

Hawks Hill and Harvest Hill Residential Zone

This area was seen by the Council as having a unique semi-rural character, surrounded and dominated by open countryside and owing more to rural than urban form. Its policy was therefore to resist any development that would create an urban character, in particular:

- infill or subdivision of plots;
- loss of trees, hedgerows and banks;
- creation of hard surfaces and walled areas.

Residential enhancement zones

These were predominantly residential areas close to town centres that, while suffering from poor layout, lack of landscaping, on-street parking and industrial and business uses, had the potential to become attractive residential areas. The policy for such areas was for new development to provide landscaping, public amenity space, off-street parking and to remove scattered employment sites. (Note the contrast with the Newtown area of Sutton where mixed uses were to be retained.)

The allocation of these zones to the 11 urban areas within the Council's boundaries is shown in Figure 5.16 (Plate 3). This was made on the basis of a survey carried out by the Council's planning officers in 1990. It took into account appeal decisions, existing densities (although in general these were not measured), nature and arrangement of vegetation, topography, car parking and the setting of buildings, both in their grounds and in their street scene. What is important for the argument here is that the zones covered almost all of the existing residential areas. Care also seems to have been taken to minimize the length of boundaries drawn along the centre lines of roads. If only the approach had been extended to non-residential land-uses.

As with the other examples, the residential character zones supplemented the general design goals in the plan which were to:

- conserve and enhance the existing residential environment;
- achieve a high standard of design and compatibility with existing forms for all types of development.

The significant point is that it was believed that these goals could not be achieved without the zones described.

The Dacorum Residential Area Character Study

Origin and development of the study

Dacorum Borough contains the towns of Hemel Hempstead, Berkhamsted and Tring. Hemel Hempstead was a post-Second World War new town, dating largely from the 1950s, which now has a population approaching 80 000 people. Berkhamsted and Tring are historic towns, of populations 18 000 and 11 000 respectively, lying astride one of the old routes from London to the north-west for road, railway and canal where it passes through the Chiltern Hills. Almost all of the area of Borough outside the main urban areas is covered by either the Metropolitan Green Belt or the Chiltern Area of Outstanding Natural Beauty, as shown by Figure 5.17.

During the 1980s significant resistance developed to the prospect of town cramming, especially among the residents of Berkhamsted and Tring. The Borough had a comprehensive local plan from 1984, the District Plan.[27] However, the Council saw the local plan, in

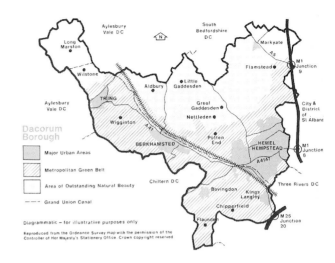

Figure 5.17 Map of Dacorum Borough Council from their Planning Information Handbook. © Crown copyright

both existing and revised forms, as an inadequate vehicle for sustaining a development control policy that would deal with issues of restraint and local character as experienced differently in the three main towns. The need for differing policies for these towns was clearest in regard to the position of Hemel Hempstead. As a large 'new town' it did not share the antique ambience of Berkhamsted and Tring but did have a historic significance of its own and one that was becoming more and more appreciated as the immediate post-war period receded into the past. It too would need protection from town cramming in a way that recognized its own particular character.

The Council also had regard to the changes that were occurring in central government policy, namely an increased awareness of the importance of environmental factors and the return to a plan-based system. It also took note of the approaches adopted by other planning authorities. It adopted the proposals made by this author's 1990 study as the theoretical base of a *Residential Area Character Study*[28] although the outcomes differed in matters of detail. This would divide the towns into design areas, analyse the character of each area and produce appropriate design objectives. The Borough has now prepared its *Borough Local Plan*[29] which replaces its previous *District Plan* of 1984. The Residential Area Character Study comes within the category of supplementary planning guidance although it is the intention to incorporate it within the *Borough Local Plan* at a later date.

POLICY 8   QUALITY OF DEVELOPMENT

A HIGH STANDARD IS EXPECTED IN ALL DEVELOPMENT PROPOSALS.

APPLICANTS WILL BE REQUIRED TO PROVIDE SUFFICIENT INFORMATION AND APPROPRIATELY DETAILED PLANS TO ENABLE THE COUNCIL TO JUDGE THE FULL IMPACT OF THE DEVELOPMENT PROPOSAL.   SPECIAL IMPACT STUDIES OR ENVIRONMENTAL ASSESSMENTS MAY BE REQUIRED IN SOME CASES.

DEVELOPMENT WILL NOT BE PERMITTED UNLESS:

(A)   IT IS APPROPRIATE IN TERMS OF:

-   LAYOUT
-   SITE COVERAGE
-   DESIGN
-   SCALE
-   BULK
-   HEIGHT
-   MATERIALS
-   LANDSCAPING
-   ON THE SITE ITSELF, IN RELATION TO ADJOINING PROPERTY AND THE CONTEXT OF LONGER VIEWS;

(B)   IT RETAINS AND SUPPLEMENTS IMPORTANT TREES AND SHRUBS, AND WHERE RELEVANT INCLUDES MEASURES TO ENHANCE THE LOCAL LANDSCAPE;

(C)   IT HARMONISES WITH THE TOWNSCAPE, DENSITY AND GENERAL CHARACTER OF THE AREA IN WHICH IT IS SET;

(D)   IT   AVOIDS   HARM   TO   THE   SURROUNDING NEIGHBOURHOOD   AND   ADJOINING   PROPERTIES THROUGH, FOR EXAMPLE, VISUAL INTRUSION, LOSS OF PRIVACY, NOISE, DISTURBANCE OR POLLUTION;

(E)   IT PROVIDES A SATISFACTORY MEANS OF ACCESS THAT WILL NOT CAUSE OR INCREASE DANGER TO PEDESTRIANS AND ROAD USERS;

(F)   THE TRAFFIC GENERATED CAN BE ACCOMMODATED ON SURROUNDING ROADS WITHOUT SERIOUS DETRIMENT TO AMENITY, SAFETY OR TRAFFIC FLOW;

(G)   IT PROVIDES SUFFICIENT PARKING AND SPACE FOR SERVICING;

(H)   IT MEETS REASONABLE REQUIREMENTS FOR ACCESS BY DISABLED PEOPLE,

(I)   IT RETAINS, DOES NOT ADVERSELY AFFECT AND WHERE APPROPRIATE   ENHANCES   IMPORTANT   LANDSCAPE, NATURAL,   ECOLOGICAL   HISTORICAL   OR ARCHITECTURAL FEATURES;

(J)   EXISTING   LOCAL   SERVICES   AND   UTILITIES (PARTICULARLY   FOR   LAND   DRAINAGE)   HAVE SUFFICIENT CAPACITY, OR MAY BE PROGRAMMED TO HAVE THAT CAPACITY; AND

(K)   IN THE GREEN BELT AND RURAL AREA, IT IS LOCATED IN SUITABLE LANDSCAPE SETTING OR IS WELL-RELATED TO AN EXISTING GROUP OF BUILDINGS.

POLICY 100   DENSITY OF DEVELOPMENTS IN RESIDENTIAL AREAS

CAREFUL   CONSIDERATION   WILL   BE   GIVEN   TO   THE DWELLING DENSITIES OF NEW HOUSING PROPOSALS. PROPOSALS FOR SITES WHICH INVOLVE AN INCREASE IN THE DWELLING DENSITY WILL BE ASSESSED WITH PARTICULAR REGARD TO THEIR EFFECT ON THE AMENITY AND CHARACTER OF THE SURROUNDING RESIDENTIAL AREA. FOR SITES AT THE EDGE OF AN URBAN AREA, SPECIAL ATTENTION WILL BE PAID TO THE EFFECT OF DEVELOPMENT DENSITY ON OPEN COUNTRYSIDE AND VIEWS; HIGH URBAN DENSITIES WILL BE AVOIDED HERE AND A SOFT EDGE TO THE COUNTRYSIDE ACHIEVED THROUGH LANDSCAPING AND RETENTION OF EXISTING TREES AND HEDGES. THERE WILL BE A PRESUMPTION AGAINST DEVELOPMENTS HAVING DWELLING DENSITY THAT WOULD ADVERSELY AFFECT THE AMENITY AND EXISTING CHARACTER OF THE SURROUNDING AREA BY REASON OF:

-   EXCESSIVE SITE COVERAGE
-   POOR DESIGN,
-   VISUAL INTRUSION
-   LOSS OF PRIVACY
-   NOISE
-   INADEQUATE LANDSCAPING
-   LOSS OF TREES, OR
-   TRAFFIC GENERATION.

IN DESIGNATED CONSERVATION AREAS, THE ISSUES OF SITE COVERAGE, DESIGN AND TREES WILL HAVE PARTICULAR RELEVANCE.   THE SITE DENSITY OF NEW DEVELOPMENT WILL BE EXPECTED TO STRONGLY CONFORM TO THAT WHICH CHARACTERISES THE CONSERVATION AREA.

Figure 5.18 Design policies from the 1994 Dacorum Borough Plan

Study methodology

The method adopted for the preparation of the Residential Area Character Study was thorough and clearly articulated. It started with the setting of parameters for the study, followed by the goal and aims. These arose from the policies of the *Borough Local Plan* on the design of the residential environment.

They are reproduced in Figure 5.18. From the goal and aims, objectives were generated for each of the three towns and from these the design area structure was obtained. This was done initially as a desktop exercise which was then revised in the light of survey work. The design areas were defined by reference to seven 'urban design qualities' and four 'neighbourhood qualities', on the basis of both the structural qualities of the urban area and the subjective perception of them by neighbourhood groups. These were as follows.

Urban design qualities

- layout and density;
- form and design of buildings, degree of continuity and spacing between them;
- incidence of spaces, both open land and amenity areas;
- provision of landscaping and planting;
- views and vistas;
- presence and type of non-residential buildings;
- car parking provision and traffic flows.

Neighbourhood qualities

- local perception of areas;
- focal points;
- landmarks;
- important edges.

The survey work required the observation by planning officers of the following qualities:

Housing	Age, design, type, height, size, layout, estimated density;
Amenity	Open space, amenity land, front gardens and forecourts, landscaping and planting, views and vistas, landmarks and focal points;
Traffic	On-street parking, off-street parking, through routes and flows;
Non-residential buildings	Type, location

From this a notion of 'area character' was developed. By considering it in the context of the study goal, the study

aims and the objectives for the relevant town, a 'policy approach' was developed for each design area. These 'policy approaches' corresponded to the design objectives recommended here. Their standard forms reflected the options to 'change', 'improve' or 'maintain' the existing character and were conceived in terms of their implications at three levels; 'layout', 'morphology within layout structures' and 'detail within plot'. They were given greater definition by setting out 'new development principles'. These were generated by considering what development would be 'appropriate' or 'inappropriate' in the light of the 'approach' and whether it should be 'encouraged' or 'controlled' in each case. The 'new development principles' for each design area were then tested by assessing their 'legitimacy' and 'practicality'.

The goals and objectives

The overall goal of the study was:

To improve, maintain and enhance the character and appearance of defined residential areas within Hemel Hempstead, Berkhamsted and Tring (Section 2.2.1)

and this was disaggregated into five general aims:

To achieve a high standard of design to buildings and spaces according to the character of defined areas within the towns.

To avoid the problems of over development and 'town cramming'.

To achieve variety in layout and design between defined areas.

To enhance and raise the visual profile of locally recognized or perceived areas.

To identify areas or parts of areas of the towns where different styles and forms of development are most appropriate. (Section 2.3.1)

Having regard to the character of the three towns, the general objectives for each of them were as follows.

Hemel Hempstead

- conserve and enhance new town structure and the concept of residential neighbourhoods;
- conserve development patterns and form in pre-new town areas;

Table 5.1 Design areas by policy type

	Hemel Hempstead	Berkhamsted	Tring
Character to be maintained or improved	19	16	12
Character to be maintained or improved with qualification	13	1	–
Changes to character proposed or allowed	2	1	–
Total	34	18	12

- improve design of development; scope for innovation and modern approaches;
- preserve and enhance high level of open spaces, amenity greens and landscaping;
- preserve long-range views across valleys and into open countryside;
- maintain low- to medium-rise nature of most residential areas.

Berkhamsted

- conserve historic core and linear nature of the town as a 'through route';
- preserve character of development appropriate to a small to medium-sized country town;
- small-scale massing in new development is most appropriate;
- maintain and improve high level of landscaping;
- maintain existing pattern of densities throughout the town;
- maintain low-rise characteristic of the town.

Tring

- conserve historic core;
- preserve character of small market country town;
- small-scale massing in new development is most appropriate;
- improve provision of public landscaping;
- maintain low-rise characteristic of the town.

For Hemel Hempstead, 34 design areas were generated and are shown in Figure 5.19. For Berkhamsted 18

were generated, and for Tring there were 12 areas. An analysis of the objectives ('approaches') for these design areas is shown in Table 5.1. It shows an overwhelming preference for a policy of no change to the existing character of nearly all parts of the three towns. This almost certainly reflects the prevailing public desire for restraint in Berkhamsted and Tring, the more historic of the three settlements. Whether it does so in late twentieth-century Hemel Hempstead will be the interesting question. More important for the reception of the policy is the contrast with the situation preceding the publication of the study. Was it understood by developers that nearly all of the three towns would have their character conserved? Was this a change of policy or just making the planners' assumptions more explicit?

There is also the issue of what is meant by 'maintaining and improving character'. This can be examined as we look closely at two contrasting design areas within Hemel Hempstead, Chaulden, and Redbourn Road. The relevant extracts from the study are reproduced in Figures 5.20–5.23.

The general format was the same for all design areas. The 'Character Appraisal' was set out under the headings of 'Housing', 'Amenity', 'Traffic' and 'Non-Residential Buildings'. Their meaning in this context can be gauged from the examples illustrated. The character appraisal was followed by the 'Policy Statement'. This contains the 'Approach' and the 'Development Principles: Scope for Redevelopment' which may be taken as equivalent to **design objectives**. The 'Development Principles' may be taken as being equivalent to **performance criteria**. However, the general style was similar to that normally employed for development plan **policies**. Character

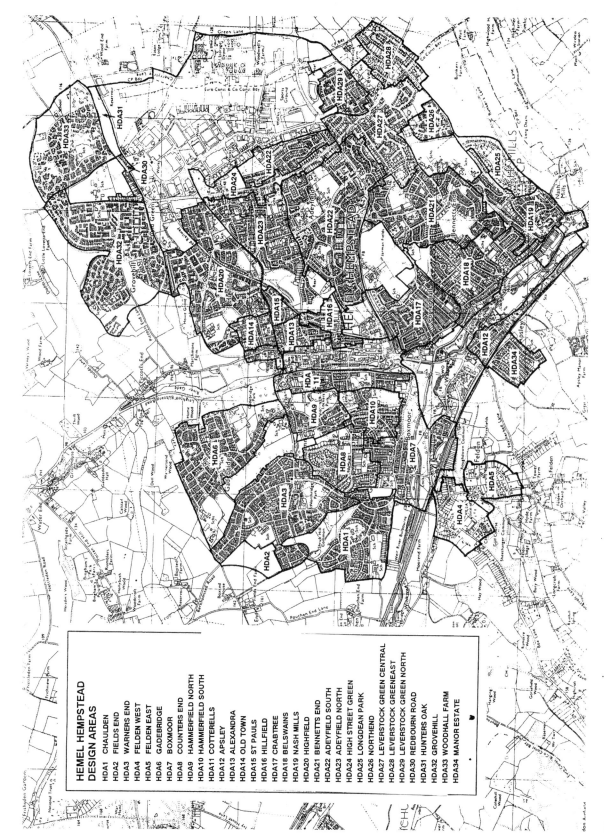

**HEMEL HEMPSTEAD
DESIGN AREAS**

HDA1   CHAULDEN
HDA2   FIELDS END
HDA3   WARNERS END
HDA4   FELDEN WEST
HDA5   FELDEN EAST
HDA6   GADEBRIDGE
HDA7   BOXMOOR
HDA8   COUNTERS END
HDA9   HAMMERFIELD NORTH
HDA10   HAMMERFIELD SOUTH
HDA11   COTTERELLS
HDA12   APSLEY
HDA13   ALEXANDRA
HDA14   OLD TOWN
HDA15   ST PAULS
HDA16   HILLFIELD
HDA17   CRABTREE
HDA18   BELSWAINS
HDA19   NASH MILLS
HDA20   HIGHFIELD
HDA21   BENNETTS END
HDA22   ADEYFIELD SOUTH
HDA23   ADEYFIELD NORTH
HDA24   HIGH STREET GREEN
HDA25   LONGDEAN PARK
HDA26   NORTHEND
HDA27   LEVERSTOCK GREEN CENTRAL
HDA28   LEVERSTOCK GREEN EAST
HDA29   LEVERSTOCK GREEN NORTH
HDA30   REDBOURN ROAD
HDA31   HUNTERS OAK
HDA32   GROVEHILL
HDA33   WOODHALL FARM
HDA34   MANOR ESTATE

Figure 5.19 Hemel Hempstead Design Area Structure

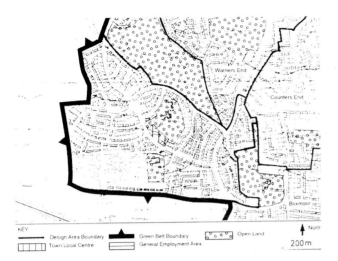

Figure 5.20 Map of the Chaulden Design Area. © Crown copyright

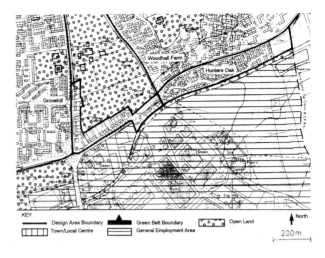

Figure 5.21 Map of the Redbourn Road Design Area. © Crown copyright

appraisal is not a technique that has been developed substantially within this book. It served the purpose in the Dacorum study of giving meaning to the objectives (the 'approach') and forming a basis for the generation of the criteria.

The most interesting aspect of the Chaulden statement was the 'Development Principles' section, see Figure 5.22, which could be taken as performance criteria for 'maintaining the defined character'. Dwelling size, shape and disposition were specified. Conformity to an architectural style was not required except in one particular part of the design area. Returning to the point made at the conclusion of the discussion of the Redbridge residential precincts, what is the difference between the Chaulden design area and a conservation area?

The Redbourn Road example was of interest because a change to the character was acceptable. The 'approach', see Figure 5.23, indicated no direction to change but the 'general points' indicated that whatever gave the place character was to be retained, namely the spacious layout and landscaping of the roads. It could be argued that it approximates to the **height-bulk envelope** objective type with the addition of the retention of the existing landscape. The disappointing feature was that the boundary was tightly drawn and passed for some distance along the centre lines of the roads, as can be seen from Figure 5.21. The Redbourn Road area borders on an industrial estate. This fact was not incorporated into either the analysis or the prescription. Changes to the industrial area could impinge on the quality of the environment in the

residential area and would, therefore, be relevant to its design policy

The principal departures from the approach recommended in Chapter 3 were:

- the study applied only to residential areas;
- advisory information was not included;
- alternative objectives were not proposed or discussed;
- objectives were not labelled as such;
- the design area boundaries sometimes followed road lines;
- roads were seldom identified as design areas;
- no urban design philosophy was made explicit.

An additional limitation of the Study was that, in common with most design guidance, it was concerned only with residential areas. As argued in Chapters 2 and 3, there is a need for guidance for other land-uses. Many of the design areas already contain shopping and educational uses and moves generating mixed uses, including small-scale office and manufacturing, in some areas would be desirable. The restriction to residential areas is the most likely case of the design area boundary problem complained of in the Redbourn Road example. What is really needed is to get away from designing by land-use category.

The most significant difference of view between the authors of the Dacorum study and the author of this book was on the matter of presenting alternative objectives. It is true that most local planning authority

HDA1: CHAULDEN

CHARACTER APPRAISAL

One of the first planned new town residential areas dating from the 1950s, typified by small dwellings closely spaced around network of narrow roads in a well landscaped setting with a local centre as a focal point.

Housing

Age: Overwhelmingly from the 1950s. Some inter-war and 1980s examples.

Design: Simple approach to overall planned area of small dwellings employing a range of finishes; use of plain brickwork and rendering common. Roof styles vary between gable ended and hipped. Orientation of buildings tends to run parallel with road although this changes to right angles at the end of certain terraces. General lack of detailing, little use of brick coursing or patterning. Original windows of simple metal frames including top hung and side hung lights. Replacements in uPVC and aluminium common. Exceptions are in:

(a) Chaulden Vale (The Poplars) development, a late 1980s development made up of standard housebuilders designs featuring a variety of treatments to the elevations, notably half-timbering;

(b) Chaulden Lane, an original line of houses dating from the inter-war period of uniform design, featuring hipped roofs and a mix of angled and rounded front bay windows.

Type: Terraced houses predominate throughout. There are some roads containing semi-detached houses such as The Lindlings and Chaulden Lane. Mix of house types in Chaulden Vale/The Poplars development from detached to cluster houses.

Height: Overwhelmingly two storey, rising to three and four storey buildings in the vicinity of the local centre on Long Chaulden, also on Northridge Way, School Row and Chaulden House Gardens.

Size: Dwellings are small throughout.

Layout: Based on planned hierarchy, with local collector roads springing from two local distributors, Long Chaulden and Northridge Way. Curvature to roads gives good serial vision. Houses have direct access onto the local distributors which feature wide grass verges with roadside hardstandings. Dwellings typically front the road although some face onto treed amenity greens; houses tend to be staggered providing richness to visual appearance; spacing between dwellings and groups of dwellings varies between close (2 m or less) and medium (2 m to 5 m). Planned layout offers few if any natural gaps for infilling.

Density: Medium, 25 - 35 dwellings/hectare

Amenity

Open space:

Well provided with land at Shrubhill Common (important nature conservation value), Chaulden School and Pixies

Hill School. Also adjacent to farmland to the west and playing fields to the south, all of which is in the Green Belt.

Amenity land:

Large presence of amenity greens with mature trees.

Front gardens and forecourts:

Mainly short front gardens with no vehicle access or hardstanding which contributes to the well landscaped appearance of area. Exceptions to this are in (a) where there are semi-detached houses (b) Chaulden Vale/The Poplars, (c) Chaulden Lane which have front gardens with access drives.

Landscaping and planting:

Mature and established throughout apart from Chaulden Vale/The Poplars.

Views and vistas:

As the area slopes downwards from north to south, good views over the Bulbourne Valley are obtained.

Landmarks and focal points:

Local centre with range of shops, public house and community centre are focal points of the neighbourhood. Brick and flint stable block with Grade II Listed octagonal tower off Chaulden Lane is an important local landmark.

Traffic

On-street parking:

Generally very high, exacerbated by little off-street provision and narrow roads.

Off-street parking:

Limited to larger houses with access drives and the Chaulden Vale/The Poplars development; some provision made in unattractive flat roofed original 1950s garage blocks.

Through routes and flows:

Road hierarchy keeps main flows to Long Chaulden and Northridge Way.

Non-residential buildings:

Grouped mainly at Chaulden local centre; Chaulden and Pixies Hill Primary Schools; Isbister Activities Centre, Chaulden Lane.

POLICY STATEMENT

APPROACH

Maintain defined character.

SCOPE FOR RESIDENTIAL DEVELOPMENT

Greenfield development:

No opportunities.

Redevelopment:

Figure 5.22 (on following pages) The Design Area Character Appraisal, Policy Statement and Development Policies for the Chaulden Design Area

Total redevelopment of plots or groups of plots is discouraged, although proposals should be assessed according to the Development Principles.

Plot amalgamation:

Discouraged

Infilling

Opportunities limited, but should be assessed according to the Development Principles.

DEVELOPMENT PRINCIPLES

Housing

Design: Variety in design acceptable; no specific style need be followed. Orientation, roof patterns and materials may vary.

Type: Terraces are encouraged. Flats acceptable in locations where height of buildings are three storeys or above. Detached houses are acceptable in Chaulden Vale/The Poplars development and along Chaulden Lane.

Height: Not to exceed two storeys, except in parts where heights are three storeys or above.

Size: Small dwellings are encouraged; buildings with large bulk and mass will be resisted.

Layout: Spacing in the medium range (2m - 5m) is expected; buildings should front onto the road or informal amenity green; building line to be followed or provided.

Density: Development must be provided in the medium density (25 - 35 dwellings/ hectare) or high density (35 - 45 dwellings/ hectare) ranges.

Amenity

Amenity land:

To be retained and not normally used for building development. In certain cases parts of these area could be used for car parking dependent on visual impact and landscaping.

Front gardens and forecourts:

The conversion of front garden areas to vehicle hardstandings is discouraged. Front gardens common in size and layout to nearby and adjacent dwellings should be provided.

Landscaping and planting:

Schemes for new dwellings will be expected to provide public landscaping to enhance the development site.

Further tree and hedgerow planting along the edge of the design area with the open countryside is encouraged.

Views and vistas:

Development proposals will be expected to preserve public views across the Bulbourne Valley to the south and open countryside to the west.

Landmarks and focal points:

Local centre in Long Chaulden and stable block with octagonal tower in Chaulden Lane should be retained.

Traffic

On-street parking:

Limit effect by provision of off-street spaces in new development proposals.

Off-street parking:

Provision of parking in communal areas (rather than front garden or forecourt areas) is encouraged; limited parking on the edge of certain amenity green may be acceptable.

Non-residential Buildings

The retention of all non-residential buildings is acceptable.

Development within the plot

Extensions:

Should be subordinate in terms of scale and height to the parent building.

Detail: No special requirements, except in the Chaulden Vale/The Poplars development where the architectural detailing on the parent building should be followed.

Curtilage buildings:

Will not normally be permitted forward of the front wall of the dwelling fronting the highway.

Means of enclosure:

No special requirements, except in the Chaulden Vale/The Poplars development where means of enclosure to front garden areas is discouraged, and should not normally exceed 1m in height.

Private landscaping:

Further planting in front garden areas is encouraged.

Conversion of dwellings into smaller units:

Discouraged.

Figure 5.22 (continued)

plans and guides do not, at present, set out alternatives. However, whereas the final approved guidance may not contain alternatives, they could be put to the public and their local councillors at a draft stage, much as alternative routes are presented for road schemes.

These criticisms must not be allowed, however, to detract from the achievements of the Dacorum study. These are:

- a systematic method starting with design goals;

HDA30: REDBOURN ROAD

CHARACTER APPRAISAL

A small corridor of small to medium sized, mainly detached to semi-detached dwellings fronted by well landscaped wide grass verges. The area, based on Redbourn Road, leads out towards open countryside but also serves as access to the residential areas of Woodhall Farm (HDA33) and Hunters Oak (HDA31).

Housing

Age: Variety, although dwellings date from the 1930s. Examples of 1980s infill and redevelopment at a higher density on St Agnells Lane.

Design: Dwellings possess very little architectural homogeneity or merit.

Type: Variety of all types.

Height: Varies between one and two storeys.

Size: Mainly small to medium sized.

Layout: A linear corridor-like area with dwellings accessed directly from the road, across grass verge areas. Spacing varies, but is typically in the medium range (2m to 5 m). There is a clear, although not totally rigid building line.

Density: Generally in the low range (15 - 25 dwellings/ha).

Amenity

Open space:

None within the area, although houses in St Agnells Lane and the northern side of Redbourn Road back onto open land between Grovehill and Woodhall Farm. Main open spaces are extensive grass verges fronting dwellings on Redbourn Road.

Amenity land:

Existing in the shape of front grass verges along Redbourn Road around 15 m deep in places.

Front gardens and forecourts:

Present on nearly all dwellings. Depth varies from 4m to around 12 m. These assist in the wide, open and well landscaped character of the area.

Landscaping and planting:

Heavy to the street appearance of Redbourn Road

Views and vistas:

Perspective views in a north-easterly direction including heavy landscaping and foliage along Redbourn Road.

Landmarks and focal points:

Cupid Green roundabout is a locally acknowledged landmark. It is the road junction between Redbourn Road and St Agnells Lane.

Traffic

On-street parking:

Practically non-existent on Redbourn Road where traffic flows are very heavy; some parking on St Agnells Lane.

Off-street parking:

Most provision made on-site in front drives.

Through routes and flows:

Redbourn Road, the B487 is an important through route to Woodhall Farm and Hunters Oak and to St Albans, Redbourn and the A5 trunk road beyond. Consequently, it is a very busy road. St Agnells Lane acts as a main access to the Grovehill neighbourhood.

Non-residential buildings:

Petrol filling station, Redbourn Road. Small church and hall, St Agnells Lane.

POLICY STATEMENT

APPROACH

Change to defined character acceptable

DEVELOPMENT PRINCIPLES

Scope for Residential Development

Greenfield development:

No opportunities.

Redevelopment:

May be acceptable according to the development principles.

Plot amalgamation:

May be acceptable according to the development principles.

Infilling:

May be acceptable according to the development principles.

General points

Housing

Design: No special requirements.

Type: Not of importance, but if redevelopment is to occur, flats are acceptable.

Height: Redevelopment up to three storeys is acceptable.

Size: An increase in the size, massing and bulk of development in the area is acceptable in cases of redevelopment.

Layout: A linear layout must be maintained with wide spacing (5 m to 10 m) in the case of redevelopment, or medium spacing (2 m to 5 m) where infill occurs, the wide grass verges and landscaping to the road must remain undeveloped. The established building line must be followed.

Density: Medium to high density (25 - 35 and 35 - 45 dwellings/ha

Figure 5.23 (on following pages) The Design Area Character Appraisal, Policy Statement and Development Policies for the Redbourn Road Design Area. © Crown copyright

respectively) is acceptable for redevelopment schemes; for infilling, a low density (15 - 25 dwellings ha) should be maintained.

Amenity

Amenity land:

The wide, deep grass verge areas fronting onto Redbourn Road must be maintained in all cases. Development proposals on these areas will not be permitted.

Front gardens and forecourts:

Where infilling is proposed, front garden areas common in size and layout to adjacent dwellings should be provided. In the case of redevelopment, front areas forward of the building line but to the back of grass verge areas may be used for vehicle parking where effective landscape screening to the road and adjacent sites is provided.

Landscaping and planting:

Existing provision should be maintained, enhanced and where necessary supplemented.

Views and vistas:

Retention and improvement of landscaping should complement and maintain attractive perspective views along Redbourn Road.

Landmarks and focal points:

No special requirements.

Traffic

On-street parking:

Acceptable along St Agnells Lane.

Off-street parking:

Provision can be by on-site private parking or communal areas.

Non-residential buildings

The redevelopment of certain non-residential building and sites may be acceptable.

Development within the plot

Extensions:

Should normally be subordinate in terms of scale and height to the parent building.

Detail: Not of importance.

Curtilage buildings:

Will not normally be permitted forward of the front wall of a dwelling fronting a highway.

Means of enclosure:

Hedging and shrub planting to the front of dwellings is encouraged.

Private landscaping:

Figure 5.23 (continued)

- complete coverage by policies of all the residential areas;
- a design area approach.

They represent a very satisfactory step forward. Their use in practice will be a significant event whose results must now be awaited.

Areas of special landscape character

Most of the discussion in this Chapter, and, indeed, the rest of the book, has used examples taken from urban situations. However, the argument has just as much application to rural settings. Unfortunately, far fewer guides were published for the countryside than for urban areas in the 1970s and 1980s although this situation did start to change for the better as the 1990s progressed. The Countryside Commission[30] drew attention to the diversity among rural areas arising from their geology, climate and farming practices and how this had produced variety in the design and materials of their forms of settlement. It proposed countryside and village 'design statements' as supplementary guidance for rural development. This advice was, however, directed mainly at new building in the countryside and to maintaining harmony with local landscapes. It did not tackle the major issue of the maintenance and enhancement of the landscapes themselves. They were subject not only to urban encroachment but also to degradation by modern farming practices, recreational use, and mineral extraction which can cause substantial changes in the aesthetics and a resulting loss in local distinctiveness. This was recognized by the *Cambridgeshire Landscape Guidelines*.[31] This publication was a joint venture between Cambridgeshire County Council, the six district councils in Cambridgeshire and the Eastern region of the Countryside Commission. It described the processes of change at work in the countryside and recommended a programme of creative renewal. To do so it employed goals, objectives, character areas and a separate consideration of control procedure, thus anticipating the argument of this book.

It set out the following 'objectives' which could be held to be equivalent to goals in the terminology used here.

FOLLOW THE GUIDELINES 21

Creating attractive village edges – the sensitive integration of new development.

Harsh, poorly integrated new development.

New development integrated by means of copse, hedgerows, trees and selected views of houses.

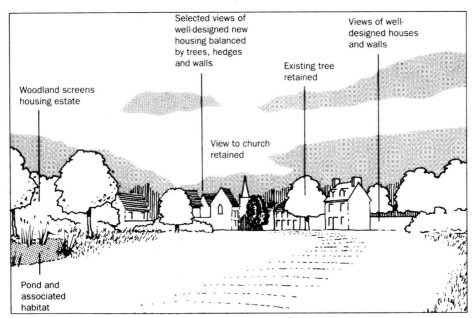

A well-designed margin between the countryside and towns and villages, combining the screening effect of woodlands and hedgerows with good architectural design and habitat gain.

Figure 5.24 The Cambridgeshire Landscape Guidelines – examples of advisory information

Footpath corridor Improvements: cross-sections.

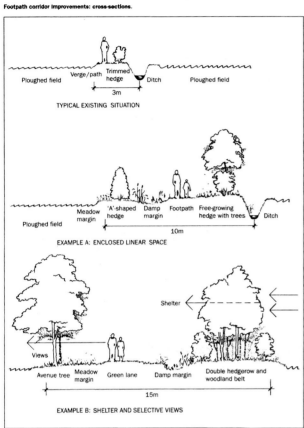

Rights of way across farmland are often obstructed by ploughed ground, narrow walking surfaces, poorly maintained or absent stiles and lack of signposting.

Important rights of way can be transformed into green lanes by the creation of landscape corridors.

Farmers and landowners can help by managing their land to allow access for walking along rights of way; guidance is available from the local authorities.

Figure 5.25 The Cambridgeshire Landscape Guidelines – examples of exploratory diagrams

1 Increase people's awareness of landscape quality.
2 Mobilize care and action amongst the main bodies who play the most active role in generating tomorrow's landscapes.
3 Improve overall visual quality and strengthen the contrasts between landscapes in different parts of the County (emphasizing a sense of place).
4 Integrate wildlife conservation into landscape action at all scales from planning at a county level, through site planning, design and management, to the detailing of 'hard' and 'soft' features at the smallest scale.

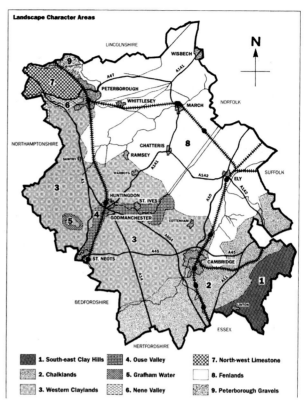

Figure 5.26 The Cambridgeshire Landscape Guidelines – Landscape Character Areas

5 Protect and enhance historic features.
6 Conserve existing features and create landmarks and 'personality' in the landscape.

It went on to lay down general 'criteria' for development (which related more closely to **objectives**, as used here) under the headings of settlements, highways (including footpaths) and rivers and drainage. Much advisory information is given. An example is illustrated by Figure 5.24. Some, as shown by Figure 5.25, show an equivalence to the idea of **exploratory diagrams**. Working on the basis of local geology, land form, land management history and towards the objective of design being responsive to locality, nine 'landscape character areas' were generated as shown by Figure 5.26. Up to ten 'policies' were listed for each area and, in the nomenclature used here, they could be seen as a mixture of **objectives** and **advice**. They were supplemented by photographs of the existing appearance of

North-west Limestone: west of Peterborough.

Stream sides, wet clay soils

Alnus glutinosa (alder) dominant, in copses, small groups and river banks.

Salix alba (white willow) sub-dominant, not in mixes.

Salix fragilis (crack willow) forms typical pollarded trees, also river banks.

Salix caprea (goat willow) scrubby copses.

Fraxinus excelsior (ash) occasional where not waterlogged.

Quercus robur (oak) occasional where not waterlogged.

Corylus avellana (hazel) occasional on stream banks if not waterlogged.

Populus tremula (aspen) in thickets, not in mixes.

Viburnum opulus (guelder rose) occasional as individuals and small groups.

Cornus sanguinea (dogwood) occasional as individuals and small groups.

Gravel soils

Alnus glutinosa (alder) dominant, copses, small groups, river banks.

Populus alba (white poplar) occasional, individuals, small groups.

Populus canescens (grey poplar) occasional, individuals, small thickets.

Salix caprea (goat willow) scrub, thickets, not mixed.

Salix alba (white willow) sub-dominant, not in mixes.

Quercus robur (oak) occasional, drier conditions, hedgerows, woodlands.

Fraxinus excelsior (ash) occasional, drier conditions, hedgerows, woodlands.

AREA 7: NORTH-WEST LIMESTONE

This compact area, a remnant of the former Rockingham Forest, has a distinct character that is typical of much of Northamptonshire rather than Cambridgeshire. It has fine landscape qualities which need careful management and selective improvements. Small villages with buildings constructed in local limestone, many with Collyweston slate roofs, are located in these low limestone hills. Mixed farming still occurs in the area, so the traditional pattern of fields enclosed by hedges or drystone walls is characteristic. Arable fields tend to be larger, and many of the hedgerows have been removed. Here the landscape can nevertheless be attractive with the large rolling fields flowing between significant woods and small copses, which provide a sense of enclosure and also frame long-distance views. There are some fine ancient semi-natural woodlands and other woods are valuable sites of nature conservation interest. A number of relic floral grassland sites, including some road verges, are also of significance. Barnack Hills and Holes and Castor Hanglands are particularly fine landscape sites with considerable nature conservation value.

PRINCIPLES FOR LANDSCAPE IMPROVEMENT AND MANAGEMENT IN THE NORTH-WEST LIMESTONE AREA

Essentially the aim is to achieve contrasts between areas of small-scale intimate landscape character full of detail and interest, and open fields sweeping amongst and enclosed by bold masses of woodlands. In the future, a greater sense of enclosure should be developed by careful woodland planting and management. Within this framework, detailed restoration and habitat creation projects relating to drystone walls and flower-rich road verges, for example, can be carried out.

1. **Management of existing woodlands:** this should aim to achieve the progressive conversion of conifer plantations to mixed broad-leaved woodlands where possible and the careful management of ancient semi-natural woodlands and re-stocking, coppicing and creation of 'edge areas' elsewhere (see Farmland Model A4b on p. 36).

2. **Road margins:** the repair of drystone walls, replanting of hedges with trees and management of verges for floral diversity would help retain or restore some of the small-scale, intimate nature of this area which has been degraded by the loss of field hedgerows.

3. **Drystone walls:** a maintenance programme is essential; new walls should be built in the traditional pattern where possible.

4. **Hedgerows:** selected hedgerows should be reinforced or managed for particularly significant impact, based upon their visual and wildlife potential. Historically significant hedgerows should be carefully conserved, and new hedges planted to emphasise the existing landscape.

5. **Footpath corridor improvements:** a number of footpaths in the area have

Figure 5.27 a

been improved by waymarking and the construction of stiles and footbridges. The next stage is to enhance the experience of walking through this landscape by the creation of features of interest, vistas and viewpoints along the key footpath corridors (see Farmland Model A7 on p. 39).

6. Planting a few carefully located woodland belts: linking woodland blocks and aligned to reinforce landforms, the woodland belts would enclose open, rolling areas of farmland and enhance significant views. If suitably sited, these may help to reduce the visual dominance of the electricity transmission lines which bisect the area.

7. Villages: most villages are attractive and have, generally, been protected from unsympathetic peripheral development. The villages are an integral part of the landscape and often combine successfully with it. Attention

should be focused on improvements to village entrances, and tree and hedge planting to subdue the visual dominance of overhead wires and screen views into the rear of properties. Ensure that key features such as avenues at Southorpe, or views to prominent landmarks such as church towers, are not lost.

8. Grasslands: some of the thinner limestone soils give marginal yields for arable crops in dry years, creating the potential to transfer them to grassland. The species-rich meadows at Barnack Hills and Holes and the superb Castor Hanglands illustrate the potential for achieving particularly fine landscape, including species-rich grassland, on limestone soils.

PLANT SPECIES GUIDELINES FOR THE NORTH-WEST LIMESTONE AREA

Mixed woodlands

Fraxinus excelsior (ash) dominant tree.

Quercus robur (oak) on deeper soils.

Prunus avium (wild cherry)

Acer campestre (field maple) glades, near edges.

Corylus avellana (hazel) main understorey shrub, glades and thickets.

Crataegus monogyna (hawthorn) near edges, thickets.

Sambucus nigra (elder) occasional, understorey and edges.

Hedgerows, woodland edges and scrub

Crataegus monogyna (hawthorn)

Corylus avellana (hazel)

CHERISH LANDSCAPE CHARACT

Prunus spinosa (blackthorn)

Acer campestre (field maple)

Rosa canina (dog rose)

Malus sylvestris (crab apple)

Trees in hedgerows

Fraxinus excelsior (ash) dominant.

Quercus robur (oak) deeper soils only.

Acer campestre (field maple)

Malus sylvestris (crab apple)

Avenues/village approaches

Quercus robur (oak)

Aesculus hippocastanum (horse chestnut)

Tilia sp. (lime)

Avenues – all as single species, not mixed.

NORTH-WEST LIMESTONE Before

Loss of hedgerows.

Poor health of hedgerow trees.

Significant woods and copses give good enclosure to broad views.

NORTH-WEST LIMESTONE After

Hedgerows replanted along road sides.

Verges managed for grass and floral diversity.

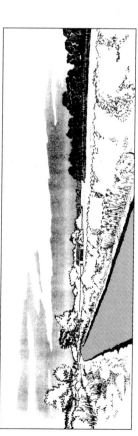

New woodlands to improve sense of scale and enclose rolling landform.

Figure 5.27 b

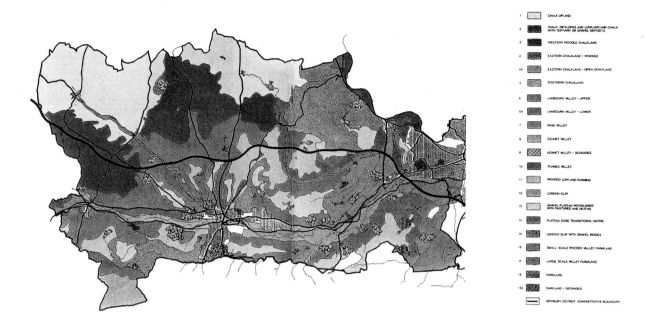

Legend:

1. CHALK UPLAND
2. CHALK DIPSLOPES AND LOWLAND AND CHALK WITH TERTIARY OR GRAVEL DEPOSITS
3. WESTERN WOODED CHALKLAND
4. EASTERN CHALKLAND - WOODED
4A. EASTERN CHALKLAND - OPEN DOWNLAND
5. SOUTHERN CHALKLAND
6. LAMBOURN VALLEY - UPPER
6A. LAMBOURN VALLEY - LOWER
7. PANG VALLEY
8. KENNET VALLEY
9. KENNET VALLEY - DEGRADED
10. THAMES VALLEY
11. WOODED LOWLAND FARMING
12. LONDON CLAY
13. GRAVEL PLATEAU WOODLANDS WITH PASTURES AND HEATHS
14. PLATEAU EDGE TRANSITIONAL MATRIX
15. LONDON CLAY WITH GRAVEL RIDGES
16. SMALL SCALE WOODED VALLEY FARMLAND
17. LARGE SCALE VALLEY FARMLAND
18. PARKLAND
18A. PARKLAND - DEGRADED

NEWBURY DISTRICT ADMINISTRATIVE BOUNDARY

Figure 5.28 Newbury District Council Landscape Character Areas (see also Plate 4)

the area and drawings showing advisory information. A list of appropriate species of vegetation was provided for each area. An example, the North-West Limestone Area, is illustrated by Figure 5.27. Aspects of implementation and control were dealt with separately, as recommended here. Some particular 'projects' were suggested and, more generally, a positive action programme for local authorities. This would be achieved through development plans, education and publicity. It was recommended that development control should utilize a range of procedures and be directed towards definite objectives.

A similar approach was taken by Newbury District Council with its *District Wide Landscape Assessment*.[32] Newbury District lies approximately 60 miles west of London and covers an area of chalk hills bisected by the River Kennett as shown by Figure 5.28. The assessment exercise was undertaken during 1992/93 to provide a significant input into a subsequent review of the authority's local plan. Systematic surveys and analysis were carried by officers of the local authority in collaboration with landscape consultants. This process resulted in the identification of 21 'landscape character areas', as illustrated by Figure 5.28 (Plate 4). Compared to the Cambridgeshire exercise, the

Newbury areas were not so strongly linked to policy considerations, being determined to a greater degree by topography and geology, and a much more intricate pattern resulted. Brief character statements, which did not cover policy implications, were appended and the links between the areas and appropriate types of vegetation were shown by means of a chart. Another chart indicated whether or not the character of each of the 21 areas was to be conserved, enhanced or have a new one created. This was followed by detailed 'landscape guidelines' which were corresponded to **objectives** in the terminology used here. Advisory information in the form of diagrams was provided for three of the areas. The most interesting example was the Kennett Valley area which was selected for both 'enhancement' and 'creation'. Its guidelines were:

9. KENNETT VALLEY-DEGRADED

- Carry out assessment of area to identify key locations for planting of new woodlands, screen planting and waterside tree planting within valley floor.
- Some larger stands of tall trees such as poplar would balance vast expanses of waterbodies created by gravel extraction.

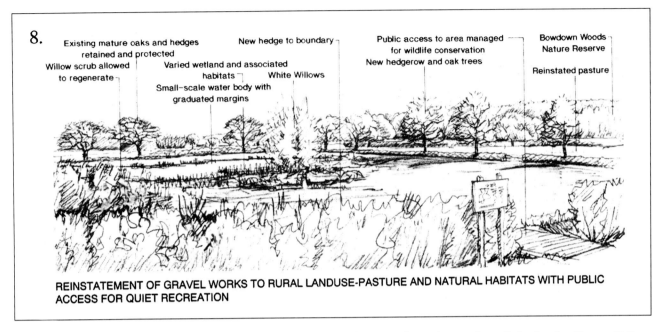

8.

Existing mature oaks and hedges
retained and protected

Willow scrub allowed
to regenerate

Varied wetland and associated
habitats

Small-scale water body with
graduated margins

New hedge to boundary

White Willows

Public access to area managed
for wildlife conservation

New hedgerow and oak trees

Bowdown Woods
Nature Reserve

Reinstated pasture

REINSTATEMENT OF GRAVEL WORKS TO RURAL LANDUSE-PASTURE AND NATURAL HABITATS WITH PUBLIC ACCESS FOR QUIET RECREATION

Figure 5.29 Newbury District Council Landscape Assessment – advisory information on the policies for the Kennet Valley Area

- Encourage management of farmland to include reinstated areas of pasture land to form new matrix of wildlife habitats which are depleted in this area.
- Maximize benefit to wildlife through creation of varied margin characteristics, depths, etc.

Figure 5.29 reproduces the diagram showing advisory information.

One of the ways in which it was intended that the assessment exercise would inform the local plan review process is of particular interest. The local plan contained 38 settlements with defined boundaries which had the effect of determining the amount of land available for new urban development. These boundaries were generally defined by the form of the urban area in two dimensions. It was proposed to examine the landscape exercise and to revise the development boundaries accordingly.

Summary and conclusions

The purpose of this chapter was to describe selected examples of planning practices in Britain that would illustrate the feasibility of the proposals made in Chapter 3. More examples had been discovered than

had been expected and the degree to which planning authorities had devised new techniques was encouraging. Not only were the Chapter 3 proposals illustrated but additional issues were highlighted.

There was evidence from surveys by others that design goals and authority-wide objectives had become commonplace in statutory development plans (and this was indeed the case with all the post-1990 plans examined in this chapter). Their presence was less pronounced in supplementary guidance and conservation studies where there often appeared to be a marked reluctance to set explicit objectives. It must also be noted that the sets of design objectives rarely encompassed a coherent and complete urban design philosophy.

The goal that had generated most of the initiatives studied was that of conservation, in the wider sense of the word. This has, no doubt, been a response to the prevailing popular mood and to the passing of the era of mass urban expansion as seen in the 1950s and 1960s. Such initiatives tended to be confined to residential areas. This was, presumably, because the area where they lived figured most prominently in people's perceptions and was the focus of such political pressure as they exerted in planning matters.

However, the most significant, if not the most frequent, examples encountered were not to do with residential areas but were concerned with the landscape of the countryside. Conservation goals were present, both explicitly and implicitly. The landscape policy documents for Cambridgeshire and Newbury district exhibited most of the features recommended – general goals, division of the whole area into smaller areas and the provision for each of them of objectives and, sometimes, advisory information. That rural situations should have generated the most important examples was something of a surprise but they were none the less worthy for that. Indeed, they illustrated the generality of the argument and showed that its utility was not restricted to urban residential areas.

Nevertheless, urban residential conservation was the issue that had generated most of the initiatives encountered, and they almost all took the form of the device termed the **residential character area**. It appeared to have been invented independently by a number of local planning authorities in London and South-east England and there was evidence that there were many more examples, to be found around the country.

The examples studied had all resulted from pressure from residents to ensure that their neighbourhood retained what they perceived to be its attractive characteristics even though it did not possess the conventionally 'historic' fabric usually associated with conservation areas. Such pressure was more likely where comparatively prosperous low-density areas were threatened with infill and redevelopment at higher density arising from the desire of even more people to move in.

The introduction of residential character areas was an attempt to ensure that a definite degree of conservation was achieved in the neighbourhoods so specified but it also carried with it the implication that this could not be achieved solely by the implementation of the authority-wide design goals and objectives contained in the development plan.

Such objectives usually required new development to be of a high standard and to be sympathetic to its surroundings. Richmond-on-Thames was one that believed its general goals and objectives had proved sufficient in practice to maintain the character, as appropriate, in all its residential areas. Although its officers had produced a detailed survey in the early 1980s that would have facilitated the generation of a design area structure, including residential character areas, they did not do so. Richmond is predominantly a high-quality (and high-income) area with an exten-

sive historic fabric. Would the same interpretation of general design policies apply in more mundane suburban areas and country towns? Would this be the view of householders in these localities?

The clear implication in those authorities that had adopted residential character areas was that outside such zones 'character', however defined, would not be conserved. In other words, although minimum standards of design of individual buildings might be required generally, the character of areas designated as residential in a local plan was liable to change according to development pressures unless further specific controls were introduced. How far would they be allowed to change and what residents could reasonably expect to happen was not made clear. In other words, what did both the general design objectives and residential designation mean in practical terms? Exactly how far could a redevelopment go before the general goals were transgressed? This was the topic that nearly all the local plans studied were most reluctant to discuss.

In the Dacorum guidance, which was not at the time of writing, part of a statutory development plan, the greater part of each of the towns included had been made subject to the objective of 'maintaining existing character'. Was 'maintaining character' a latent objective in the other authority's plans? In other words, would all really like extensive coverage by residential character area if only this were politically (in central government terms) feasible?

A linking argument could be that what is really missing is control of residential densities. If they were specified the precise position on the redevelopment of each neighbourhood would be known. Chiltern District attempted this but were encouraged to retreat from it. However, as was argued in Chapter 2, density is an output not an input and density controls are no substitute for a comprehensive urban design philosophy. This is what is really missing even from the most sophisticated examples of design control policy. Although the specification of degrees of conservation is welcome, it is policies for directing change that should be the concern of town and country planning.

Arising from the designation of residential character areas was the need to define the character to be conserved in each case. The attempt was not always made. Often only very general and brief descriptions were provided. Rarely were criteria or advisory information provided. Where they were, as in Sutton and Dacorum Boroughs, a uniform system did not emerge.

Nevertheless, there were important points of commonality, such as the recognition of the important role of trees and other vegetation and the importance of controlling building types in their settings as opposed to just the aesthetics of individual buildings. Defining character in such terms still left much scope for the initiative of the architect. Such progress was encouraging but there was still a long way to go.

Notes and references

1. Dept. of Environment (NI) (1987) *Queen's Conservation Area*, Belfast: HMSO.
2. London Borough of Richmond (1989) The Riverside. Extract from *Barnes Green Study, Conservation Area No. 1*.
3. J. Hendry *et al.* (1986) *Conservation in Belfast*, Dep.t of Architecture and Planning, Belfast: Queen's University.
4. S. J. Gould (1992) *Design Policy in London's Unitary Development Plans*. Unpublished MPhil thesis, Dept. of Land Management and Development, Reading University. The findings of this work are summarized in Gould (1992) London's unitary development plans: design policy and control. *Urban Design Quarterly*, 44, 11–16.
5. Royal Town Planning Institute (1993) *The Character of Conservation Areas*. Commissioned Study from Chesterton Consulting and University of Central England, London: RTPI, Appendix E.
6. The unitary plans were required by Section 13 of the Town and Country Planning Act 1990, amended by Section 27 of the Planning and Compensation Act 1991. The government guidance was Dept. of Environment (1988) *Regional Guidance for the Southeast*, PPG 9 London: DoE, revised in 1993 (draft), and *Strategic Policy Guidance for London* (1986), revised as RPG3 (1989) London: DoE. RGP3 was based on advice from the Southeast Regional Planning Conference (1990) *A New Strategy for the Southeast*, RPC 1789.
7. LPAC (1988) *Strategic Planning Advice for Greater London*.
8. Buckinghamshire County Council (1990) *County Structure Plan*, Aylesbury: Buckinghamshire CC.
9. Hertfordshire County Council (1992) *County Structure Plan Review*. Hertford: Hertfordshire CC.
10. Essex County Council (1957) *Development Plan for Metropolitan Essex*, Written Statement and County Map, Chelmsford: Essex CC.
11. London Borough of Redbridge (1994) *Unitary Development Plan*, Ilford: LB of Redbridge.
12. Officer's view quoted in a letter from the Borough Planning Officer to the London Regional Office of the Department of the Environment, 23 July 1993.
13. London Borough of Redbridge, Minutes of Council, 15 October 1987.
14. Before the 1990 Town and Country Planning Act, the view was that only listed buildings and buildings in conservation areas were subject to demolition control as demolition was not development The Courts subsequently held that demolition was development. This was confirmed by the 1992 Planning and Compensation Act but the General Development Order was amended in 1993 to make demolition permitted development for all properties except for private dwelling houses. There is therefore no control over the demolition of non–residential buildings.
15. London Borough of Sutton (1978) *Living in Sutton, Report of Studies*.
16. London Borough of Sutton (1981) *Living in Sutton, Sutton District Plan*.
17. London Borough of Sutton (1988) *Sutton Local Plan*.
18. London Borough of Sutton (1994) *Unitary Development Plan Deposit Draft*.
19. London Borough of Richmond (1981) *Environmental Character*, District Plan Topic Study Report No. 7.
20. London Borough of Richmond (1985) *District Plan*.
21. London Borough of Richmond (1992) *Unitary Development Plan*.
22. Interviews with the author during 1994.
23. Chiltern District Council (1990) *The Draft Local Plan for Chiltern District (except Chesham Town Centre and Waterside)*, and (1991) *The Draft Chesham Local Plan*.
24. Chiltern District Council (1992) *The Local Plan for Chiltern District (except Chesham Town Centre and Waterside), Inspector's Report on Objections to the Local Plan*.
25. Chiltern District Council (1993) *The Local Plan for Chiltern District, (except Chesham Town Centre and Waterside)*, and (1993) *The Chesham Local Plan*.
26. Wycombe District Council (1994) *Wycombe District Local Plan*.
27. Dacorum Borough Council (1984) *District Plan*, Hemel Hempstead: Dacorum BC.
28. Dacorum Borough Council (1995) *Residential Area Character Study, Discussion Draft*, Hemel Hempstead: Dacorum BC.
29. Dacorum Borough Council (1995) *Dacorum Borough Local Plan*, Hemel Hempstead: Dacorum BC.
30. Countryside Commission (1993) *Design in the Countryside*, Technical Paper CCP418, Cheltenham: Countryside Commission.
31. Cambridgeshire County Council (1991) *Cambridgeshire Landscape Guidelines – A Manual for Change*, Cambridge: Cambridgeshire CC in association with Granta Editions. The publication is available from Granta Editions, Cambridge.
32. Newbury District Council with Landscape Design Associates (1993) *District Wide Landscape Assessment – A Summary*. Newbury: Newbury DC and Peterborough: Landscape Design Associates.

Chapter 6

COMMUNICATING DESIGN POLICY

So far the argument has concerned the status, structure and use of design policy. There remains the issue of its means of communication. In developing the proposed method, in particular the four-way split, the intention was to make the design plan something that could be used in negotiations with lay parties – applicants, local politicians and the public at large. However, this effort would be of no avail if the policies could not be communicated to these people in a manner which would enable them to understand unambiguously and respond in kind. Negotiation is at least a two-way process and its efficiency is dependant upon effective communication.

Selected requirements for effective communication have been brought out in Chapter 3. The distinction between **performance criteria** and **advisory material** implies that the parties to the negotiations understand clearly what is compulsory, what is optional and what is left completely open. Indeed, such a distinction can be said to be fundamental to all design guidance. The problem is that it can be difficult to achieve in practice because of the large amount of information contained within the physical environment. Any representation of it must require selection and the process of selection may involve unintended bias, unintended omissions of matters taken for granted or the inclusion of extraneous detail into which unintended messages can be read.

The media available

Written statements

Although not directly visual in content, written statements are commonly used in development plans for policies relating to the physical environment. They are robust for legal purposes but leave a great deal to the imagination in terms of design content. This can have both good and bad consequences. Written statements can have the advantage of clarifying the compulsory requirements without needing to show a particular design solution. A possible example would be, 'the space between the buildings shall be for pedestrian circulation only and shall be provided with seating and trees'. Certain specific requirements are laid down but no other detail is given and the scope for the designer to specify paving, seating and landscaping is left open. However, whereas a written statement of this type can be ideal for the **criteria** it is of little use for the **advisory material** as it does not contain detailed information. To attempt to introduce the detail is to confront the problem that the written statements are a very inefficient means of conveying complexity in comparison with visual media. It is not only the number of words but the legalistic language needed in attempts at definition that can ultimately create a cumbersome and unwieldy text.

Diagrams and drawings

It was suggested in Chapter 3 that diagrams can be useful for exploring and developing the performance criteria. However, they were not used in the examples for any wider purpose and there can be problems if they are applied in a broader context. It is true that they can be the only means when on site of conveying visual ideas speedily from person to person but this will usually be at a fairly elementary level. The problem occurs when more detail is required, particularly with regard to advisory material. The rapid production of detailed sketches requires much skill and it can be difficult for the lay person to respond in kind.

The lay person is at even more of a disadvantage when confronted with architects' plans and elevations. These are technical documents that result from the mathematical projection of the shape of a building on to a plane surface and are not views that can be seen in reality. Although they have an essential role in architecture and building processes, they are not a suitable medium for conveying design control policy. They are, on the contrary, one of the main obstacles to doing so.

Artists' impressions also pose fundamental problems. They may, at first sight, appear to provide a means of communicating the impact of proposed development to a lay public but they are both expensive to produce and are not open to an interactive response. Moreover, they are of almost legendary subjectivity and are often the subject of accusations of bias.

Photographs

At first sight, photographs of existing urban form seem an ideal means of conveying the advisory material, as they can give a direct visual representation of all the necessary detail in a realistic manner. Many alternative views can be produced, annotations made to the images and photo-montages created to marry the proposal to its context. However, the problem is that too much detail is conveyed. The viewer may not be able to distinguish between the details that are essential and those that are not. There is also the criticism that all photography contains an element of subjectivity, even bias, as views can be chosen to show a subject in a flattering or disadvantageous light.

Three-dimensional scale models

Three-dimensional scale models may also appear, at first sight, to have many advantages. The direction of view is not fixed, the required level of detail can be shown and, in principle, the model can be altered with parts being moved around as required. Nevertheless, such modules have significant limitations, one initial problem being the labour and skills, and therefore cost, needed to produce them. Although the technology has

been available for millennia, they have never achieved widespread use in town and country planning for this reason alone. More significantly, there is a subtle distortion in decision-making caused by such models which arises from the difficulty in viewing them from the position of a user at ground level. It is true that a modelscope can be used to produce this effect and, when combined with a gantry and video camera, a video recording of a walk-through can be obtained. However, such procedures are cumbersome and expensive and the temptation is to view the model from above. When seen in this way, items such as houses and gardens that are significant at human scale can seem insignificant (or, at least, undramatic). On the other hand, large buildings such as offices or blocks of flats may take on a sculptural significance that, although pleasing for some designers, may be overwhelming in its impact on users at ground level. Some hold that much of the popularity of high-rise buildings during the second half of the twentieth-century can be attributed to this effect.

Notwithstanding these criticisms, the British Planning for Real movement has encouraged lay people to amend and develop proposals by manipulating three-dimensional models. Promoted by the Neighbourhood Initiatives Foundation, considerable success has been reported. Such models are used in combination with other decision-making techniques, to enable people affected by a new development to influence its outcome.[1] For example, tenants of a housing estate can manipulate small model houses and shops in order to illustrate their views on their best location and to explore and extend these views on a trial and error basis. It is not so much the visual impact that is being considered as the functional arrangement of the buildings. The model enables this to be represented in a way that people can readily take in. There is, fortunately, now a way of combining these features of **interaction** and **accessibility** with the realistic representation of visual impact. This is the use of computer visualization.

Computer visualization

Computer visualization would appear to offer the solution to most of the problems in communication referred to above. Highly realistic colour perspective images of proposed development can be produced by computer hardware and software that is readily available on the retail market at affordable prices. The level of detail can be adjusted easily according to the purpose of the task in hand. The position of the viewer is almost infinitely variable. Moreover, the images can be altered quickly and interactively as negotiations proceed. The principal cost is the operator time necessary to input the data and model the images. Fortunately, the direction of technological change in software development is towards greater user friendliness and developments in the automatic scanning of data should reduce labour costs in the long term. Even at the present time, the skills and training necessary to produce computer visualizations do not approach that required for manual drawing and model making. It is a technical capability that can be made available to all planning agencies.

The use of computer visualization

Computer visualization is potentially the most effective medium for conveying design control ideas in negotiation.

It does, however, have its limitations and, as with all media, these must be recognized if effective use is to be made of the technique. It is important to distinguish it from **computer-aided design** and from the use of visualization to present proposals to the public. What is being discussed here is the use of computers to improve two-way communication in pursuit of more effective decision-making, especially greater participation by the public, one of the principal arguments of this book. There has, unfortunately been much less research and practice on this particular topic than for computer-aided design. Some British planning authorities have had some success but they have been isolated ones. Research in Britain has been conducted by the author[2] and dates from 1987 onwards.

The initial work enabled a number of planning authorities to asses the visual impact of large developments. In one case, all of the buildings surrounding a large town centre site were modelled. The variations in the possible design of the proposed use were then explored.[3] However, greater significance for its application to design control was to be found in small-scale examples, such as domestic extensions, where negotiation between planning officers, applicants and their professional agents were involved. In 1991 two examples of such proposals were studied. The first was a house extension that was visualized from the architects' plans submitted with the application in order to support the position of the planning authority. A high degree of realism was employed and this included cast shadows as overshadowing was one of the points at issue. The planning committee refused the application and their decision was upheld at a subsequent appeal. The computer-generated images were shown to the committee and sent to the inspector who determined the appeal. The committee members commented that they found them useful as they enabled members who had not seen the site to participate in the discussion. However, the applicant's architects objected to their use, raising a number of objections and criticisms, particularly on the overshadowing issue, where they maintained that a more realistic result could be obtained by means of a protractor and calculations.

They also queried the **objective** status of the visualization on the basis that judgment had to be used on what items are included or excluded, and maintained that architects' perspective drawings in colour could give a more objective impression, in appropriate circumstances. They believed that computer visualization had a role in the presentation of projects but not any **special** or **independent** role in the control process. What was learnt from this experience was that, although successful from the planning authority's point of view, visualization had been shown to be lacking in general acceptance when used to support only one part in an adversarial situation. In particular, although the images had been circulated to the participants, they did not come together at any stage to negotiate using the computer interactively.

An opportunity to use visualization interactively in a routine development control context arose soon afterwards. This example related to the extension of a house over a garage. There had been unsuccessful negotiations between the applicants' builder and the planning officer regarding the design using the builder's scale drawings and the planning officer's pencil sketches. The issue was referred to the research project and some initial visualizations were prepared. A negotiating session around the computer was subsequently arranged and was attended by one of the applicants, her builder and a planning officer. A visualization of the existing and neighbouring houses (Figure 6.1a), not at the highest degree of realism, was agreed by all

(a)

(b)

(c)

(d)

Figure 6.1 Visualization of stages of negotiation for a house extension
Original situation a
Builder's proposal b
Planning officer's proposal d
Applicant's proposal d

the parties to form an acceptable basis for negotiation. The merits of the proposals from the builder (Figure 6.1b), the planning officer (Figure 6.1c) and some other suggestions were debated without agreement. The applicant then made a suggestion of her own which had not been previously considered. This was visualized on the spot and became the agreed concept (Figure 6.1d). Revised plans were subsequently approved by the planning authority and the extension constructed. All the parties commented favourably on the effectiveness of the technique. What was especially significant was that a lay woman had been able to put forward her own proposal, which had not been previously considered, and have it accepted by design professionals.

The effectiveness of computer visualization as an interactive medium had been illustrated. It had become clear that realism was a relative concept. Its level should be determined by balance between the requirements of the negotiating parties and the cost. It was uneconomic to model to a very high level of realism. What, though, if the required level of realism was higher than could be afforded? What were the financial implications for their routine use in a planning office? The cost of visualizing very large developments should fairly fall upon the developer. Some already do this for presentational purposes. Most large schemes are now designed on the computer using programs that facilitate the production of perspectives. For residential extensions costs could be kept down by having a library in the computer of standard house types and standard extensions, much as they are commonly illustrated in design guides.

The question arose of whether it would be economic to model, at some expense, the whole of an important part of a town, say a shopping centre or conservation area, so that minor alterations to it could then be visualized quickly and cheaply. An opportunity to test this idea occurred when a model of Colchester High Street, Essex, was commissioned for the assessment of a proposed traffic scheme. This required a 'medium' level of realism, as shown by Figure 6.2a, which was effective for its purpose. However, the planning officers considered that the only development control use at this level of realism would be the assessment of the bulk and overshadowing of a large new building; something that occurred very rarely in this part of town. It would not be suitable for the assessment of changes to

shopfronts and listed buildings. As an experiment, a series of simulations at a high level of realism was produced to illustrate the stages of negotiation of a shopfront issue. Examples from it are shown by Figures 6.2b–6.2e. This confirmed the effectiveness of the use of visualization as a negotiating tool but there remained questions concerning the cost.

The principal findings from the research were as follows:

1. All the participants were impressed with the quality of image that the current hardware and software could produce. The realism of the images depended on the human resources that could be employed and, in general, was found to be adjustable to the requirements of the task in hand.

2. The question of objectivity and realism was an important one There was a strong argument for obtaining the agreement of all parties involved to the level of realism in the visualization of the existing development before proceeding to the negotiation.

3. There was no problem producing images of development on small sites within the time scale required by the development control process.

4. The modelling of extensive background features was not found to be necessary when dealing with the issues affecting development on small sites.

5. An important advantage of computer visualization appeared to be its ability to bring the 'site' into the office. The way that it could enable people without a detailed knowledge of the site to participate in discussions was frequently cited as a major innovation.

6. Photomontages were not of great use because of the loss of the ability to modify the image interactively.

7. There was direct evidence of the advantage to lay people of visualization. The Chelmsford example, in particular, illustrated how it could enable an applicant to make a decisive suggestion that may not otherwise have come forward.

8. There was also confirmation of the assistance that computer visualization could give to professionals engaged in the design process by providing feedback on the appearance of their proposals.

9. The principal problem was the cost in staff time. It was likely that this would be reduced by further technological innovation.

(a)

(b)

(c)

(d)

(e)

Figure 6.2 Visualization of Colchester High Street, Essex, for the assessment and presentation of a traffic scheme and for the representation of the stages of negotiation of a proposal for a new shopfront
Colchester High Street a
Original shopfront b
First proposal c
Second proposal d
Agreed scheme e

Objectivity and realism in visualization

The issue of **objectivity** is central and deserves further discussion. A central component of the argument for the use of computer visualization in planning control is that it should be seen to be independent of the positions of all the negotiating parties. It can provide them with a common point of reference, a means for resolving disputes on points of fact and a basis for an independent test against which the participants can measure the strength of their arguments. However, this is not an assertion that meets with universal agreement and there are, indeed, some important issues to be debated.

111

Let us take one extreme on the scale of objectivity, the artist's impression. This is normally held to be the epitome of the subjective image: very much a device for advocacy and little use as independent evidence. Why is this so? The subjectivity arises where, in the course of producing the drawing, the artist, who is employed to represent the interests of developer, is confronted with choices which require judgment to be exercised on the basis of opinion and interpretation. In attempting to break down the components of the subjectivity the following points of choice and decision can be identified:

1. a single viewpoint (or a very limited number) is selected to show the proposal to advantage; unflattering views need not be made available;
2. perspectives, where not obtained geometrically, may be liable to distortion;
3. lighting, especially sunlight, and consequent shading and shadows may be exaggerated or underplayed for good effect and only ideal conditions may be shown;
4. the detail in which buildings can be shown can be selected for effect;
5. background buildings, parts of buildings, paving, street furniture and landscaping can be included or excluded to create the desired effect;
6. the appearance of materials to be used can be enhanced or played down as required.

The argument for the objectivity of computer visualization rests primarily on the first three qualities:

1. the viewpoint is infinitely variable and can be selected by any party;
2. perspectives are calculated to such accuracy that it is possible to fit a computer image on top of a photograph of the same site taken to the same visual parameters;
3. the lighting is variable in colour, intensity and direction and can be adjusted to positions requested by any party.

In addition, shadows can be calculated exactly and can be checked for accuracy by comparison with those thrown by existing buildings.

The argument for objectivity relates to the independence of the observer. Any desired image can be requested by any party and all will be obtained on an equivalent basis. For the other qualities listed for the artist's impression, however, the matter becomes more complicated. It could be argued that the increasing ability of information technology to produce photorealistic images could provide the solution. The test could be: 'if the computer image is indistinguishable from a photograph for the existing situation then the modelled proposals must be completely objective'. Unfortunately, there is the immediate objection that photographs incorporate outside judgment and therefore, a level of subjectivity. There are also more general problems with the 'realism equals objectivity' argument. Questions of level of detail and inclusion and exclusion of items will continue to exist for two important reasons.

Firstly, the economics of the visualization process imply that it is not practicable to model to the maximum available level of realism. For example, if cast shadows are the only issue then why spend time and money modelling the colour and texture of the brickwork?

Secondly, negotiations concerning development proposals frequently occur at a stage where none of the details has been incorporated in the design, let alone agreed. To come to arbitrary decisions on, for example, such matters as choice of colours, building materials and landscaping merely in order to achieve the highest degree of realism could confuse the deliberations by raising points prematurely or even go so far as to create a misleading impression. (It is not being suggested here that there would be a deliberately subjective input, merely that confusion could result.)

In practice, therefore, users will need to make decisions about what items should be included and the level of detail to which they should be modelled. The decisions thus made should relate to the purpose of the exercise and will include an element of subjective judgment. The **objective** quality will lie, as referred to in the test results above, in the way the images are used and in the basis upon which the negotiations are conducted. If all the parties agree, at the outset, that they have confidence in the ability of the hardware and software to produce a usefully realistic representation of the existing situation, then the subsequent visualization of the proposals will command an objective status on the grounds that it has been deduced from a common position. The argument for the objectivity of computer visualization rests, therefore, in part on the independence and validity of the algorithms employed

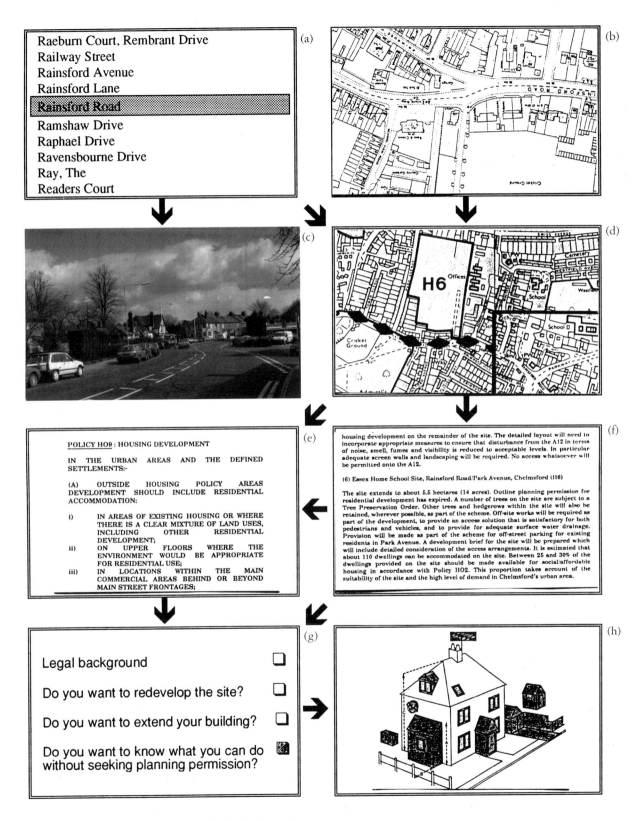

Figure 6.3 A demonstration of multimedia local plan linkages

within the working of the programs and in part on the way visualization is applied in the modelling and decision-making process.

The arguments above lead also to the solution of the more general problem of the level of realism to be modelled. The concept of total realism is open to criticism as it is practically unachievable. Realism is a relative concept. In theory, finer and finer detail of the components of a building could be modelled given sufficient computer power and operator time, and every door handle, keyhole and grain in the wood could be shown. However, resources are most unlikely to be available on a scale that would make this a practical proposition. It is suggested, on the basis of the arguments above, that the balance between realism and economics is determined by the negotiated agreement between the parties involved.

Multimedia

Although computer visualization is clearly the key to the communication of design control policy in a form suitable for use in negotiations, all the media discussed above will continue to exist and many are likely to be in play at the same time. In addition, video recordings of development sites made by planning authorities, architects and members of the public are likely to become more and more common. Computers can offer multimedia facilities whereby text, pictures, video recordings, audio recordings and computer-aided design files can all be held in the same machine and be displayed on one screen at the same time. Hypermedia links can enable the user to move directly from a point of reference in one file in one medium to a reference to the same subject in another file in a different medium. This is achieved without the need to start again at the beginning of each file and examine the index.

To imagine the possible application and advantages of these facilities, the process of making and considering an application for planning permission can be taken as an example. An applicant could collect from the planning office a pre-recorded disc for replaying on home equipment. The disc could contain a copy of the development plan for the area, essential legal information and a template into which to enter the proposals. An architect could copy a computer-aided-design file directly on to the disc for examination by the planning officers on their own equipment. A lay applicant could copy on to the disc some scanned images of drawings, a home video of the site or a sound recording of a commentary on the proposals. The disc could be replayed by the planning officers in the presence of the applicants and their professional advisers and could be used interactively in the negotiations.

Multimedia facilities can also make development plans far more accessible to the public. It is difficult for a lay person to see how a plan could affect his or her own property or any other particular site in which they may be interested. To do so normally requires reading several chapters and, hopefully, understanding them. For example, residential development could be affected by parts of the chapters entitled 'housing', 'design and the environment' and, say for parking matters, 'transport'. The internal structure of each chapter can be complex and, to the lay person, full of jargon. For the householder who wishes to erect, say, an extension with garage it can be difficult to find and comprehend the particular policies that apply to this particular proposal. A multimedia computer based development plan could largely remove this problem. Figure 6.3 shows an extract from a demonstration of the operation of such a plan.[4] The user may find an address from the list shown in Figure 6.3a or, alternatively, navigate over a map, as shown by Figure 6.3b, to find the desired site. Photographs of the area can be displayed, as shown by Figure 6.3c. Once the site has been selected, the relevant part of proposals map from the local plan is automatically displayed as shown by Figure 6.3d. By selecting the site or adjacent land the user can reveal the policies and proposals appertaining to the plot in question as shown by Figures 6.3e and 6.3f. By selecting the appropriate 'buttons', as seen in Figure 6.3g, subsidiary policies, and relevant legal background can be accessed. Permitted development rights can be investigated through the medium of three-dimensional diagrams, as shown by Figure 6.3h.

Again, it is the ability of the lay person to play a full role in the decision-making process and the consequent avoidance of misunderstandings that is the important result.

Decision support and expert systems

Since the late 1980s there has been much development work, if not practical use, of the means by which information technology can give direct assistance to operational decision-making, particularly for professional tasks concerned with the development process. These are generally known as **decision support systems**. They take advantage not only of the many applications, such as word processing, spreadsheets and mathematical modelling, that information technology provides but also the many media, such as text, graphics and sound as described above. It can incorporate them into one system that can be used interactively as required. The system can be tailored to a particular task enabling the support to be obtained where, when and in the manner required. The development control packages common in British practice could be said to represent a very elementary and simplistic application of this idea. They do not really approach the true idea of the decision support system because they do not engage the decision-making process in any active sense. This is very much the province of a separate aspect of decision support, the **expert system**.

Although with a separate development history and based upon different postulates, some authors[5] believe that the two ideas are now convergent. An expert system is more narrowly focused and attempts to replicate aspects of the human decision-making process within the computer. The idea is not just to answer questions with facts, as in a reference book, but to suggest lines of enquiry to the user and to present alternative solutions thereby actively assisting in the solution of the problem. However, in spite of over ten years of development there is, at the time of writing, hardly any use of expert systems in the development process in general, or town planning practice in particular, and the more general decision support systems are encountered only in the most elementary form. One reason for this may be that potential users are waiting for readily available, cheap and user-friendly packages that are tailored to small scale practical uses. In other words, they are not over-ambitious in their scope. The history of the application of information technology indicates that once this happens then demand takes off and eventually more and more sophisticated versions are then marketed.

The three-dimensional design plan

Multimedia, visualization and decision support systems all come together in the three-dimensional computer-based model. This model can be seen as the frame on

Figure 6.4 Three–dimensional computer–based model of the City of Bath

which the visual and textual examination of policies is hung in order that such an investigation is accessible to the public in a direct and interactive manner. Three-dimensional models have been constructed for the central areas of several British cities, notably Glasgow, Edinburgh[6] and Bath, in chronological order. The Bath model is illustrated by Figure 6.4. In Bath[7] work was underway at the time of writing to hang an expert system developed by Southampton University on the model of the city developed by Bath University. The purpose was to enable the user to navigate in three-dimensions to locate a building and then to examine the documentation relating to it. This project will lay the groundwork for the computer-based multimedia development plan.

The most impressive long-term innovation here is likely to be the use of virtual reality. On the desktop, virtual reality enables the user to move around the simulated environment on the monitor screen at will and in a continuous manner. In 1992, the Tyne and Wear Development Corporation commissioned a virtual reality model of the Newcastle Quayside.[8] A desktop facility was used to walk-through and fly through the proposed development in real-time. This exercise provided valuable feedback for the designers. More significantly, monthly meetings were held between local representatives, developers and councillors at which the virtual reality system was used to aid the discussion of all aspects of the scheme. It thereby enabled lay parties to make suggestions and have changes made.

Although the desktop facility makes it easy to navigate in the visualized environment and thus increases the ease of use, the future belongs to the fully immersive three-dimensional version. Subjects wearing masks, gloves and earphones that are on-line to a computer may not be appropriate for planning control purposes but the advantages of seating a planning committee inside a room with 360° projection for a 'drive around' a computer-generated model of their town will be clear. Proposed buildings could not only be viewed from all angles but could be altered interactively. Moreover, individual members would be able to 'explore' the town independently. These innovations would bring both the public and the participants in the process of negotiation ever closer to experiencing the true impact of proposed development.

Summary: towards the responsive development plan

Interaction with the public, especially the potential users of a proposed development, is the only effective way of testing design policy and developing it further. This has, arguably, been the experience of the British Planning for Real movement.

The problems in communicating a design plan can be summarized as follows:

- the difficulty set out at the beginning of this chapter regarding the public's understanding of the media in current use;
- the difficulty claimed by some planning officers in producing policy that would cover the myriad of possible eventualities;
- the accommodation of the advisory material;[9]
- the handling of design goals that may have a cultural, even specifically literary, content.

The advent of the technology discussed in this chapter can facilitate the accommodation all the points made above and would enable the user to interact with the plan. A disc containing a planning application template, legal and development plan information which could be interrogated by a micro-computer has been suggested. This idea could form part of a more general and powerful system whereby a multimedia computer based development plan was interrogated

using a decision support system. This plan would contain:

- all the design goals and objectives for the plan area;
- the performance criteria for the objectives explained by three-dimensional diagrams;
- a very large number of alternative designs consistent with objectives, in three-dimensions and indicating building materials;
- written statements of the control processes to be used;
- access to legal texts.

The decision support system would enable the user to find answers to questions originally conceived in lay terms. Hypermedia facilities would permit direct links between reference points and visualization would enable all appropriate matters to be dealt with in pictures of three-dimensional objects. Starting from a particular site, relevant policies could be immediately accessed, legal questions answered and possible ways of proceeding suggested. Furthermore, the implications of wider cultural goals could be indicated by direct reference to examples from literature or films.

All this is possible within the limits of existing technology. It is only resource limitations, particularly staff time, that prevent it being made operational. It must be stressed that this proposal is put forward not to generate futuristic excitement but to show how the obstacles to truly responsive planning are not ultimately practical ones, as the technical problems can, given sufficient resources, be overcome. Indeed, the increasing rate of change in information technology implies that there may not be a long wait before such facilities become affordable in the ordinary office. The same can be said for the following suggestion, however fanciful it may seem to the reader. Given sufficient computer power and staff time for data input, it would be possible to model almost all of an urban area in a computer and then build the development plan policy into this model. It would then be possible for the public not only to interrogate the plan but also to insert proposals into it on an interactive basis (without necessarily saving them) and thereby test them directly against the policies. Visual comparisons could be made and warning messages perhaps received. The entire plan system would become an aid to direct negotiations and **planning for real** would truly have arrived.

Notes and references

1. See e.g. T. Gibson (1991) This neighbourhood plan is different. *District Councils Review*, January, 16–17.

2. The initial publication was A. C. Hall (1988): Computer visualisation for design and control. *The Planner*, 74(10), 21–5. A full report of the research in the 1990–92 period is available as A. C. Hall (1992) *Computer Visualisation: An Investigation of its Application to the Control of Urban Design*, Chelmsford: Anglia Polytechnic. A shorter account was published as A. C. Hall (1993) The use of computer visualisation in planning control: an investigation of its utility in selected examples. *Town Planning Review*, 64(2), 193–212. Work on Colchester, Essex, was published as A. C. Hall (1995) Visual reality. *Planning Week*, 3(11), 16–17.

3. Work was also undertaken on lay reaction to building colour. A computer image of a block of flats was displayed to a lay audience. Its colour scheme was changed progressively and the reaction of the participants recorded. The results revealed somewhat conservative tastes, perhaps unsurprisingly, but it was the technique itself that was significant.

4. A. C. Hall, D. King and M. Woodroffe (1994) The potential of multimedia for urban management. *17th Urban Data Management Symposium*, Helsinki University of Technology, Finland.

5. For this point, a general overview and further reading see A. Rodriguez-Bachiller (1991) Expert systems in planning: an overview. *Planning Practice and Research*, 6(3), 20–5.

6. M. Grant (1993) ISSUE (Interactive Software Systems for the Urban Environment). In U. Fleming and S. Van Wyk (eds), *CAAD Futures '93*, Proceedings of the 5th International Conference on CAAD Futures, Pittsburgh, Amsterdam: Elsevier, pp. 557–564 and M. Grant and I. Paterson (1994) Urban Modelling. In T. Maver and J. Petrie (eds), *The Virtual Studio*, Proceedings of the 12th European Conference on CAAD, Glasgow, pp. 135–139.

7. A. Day (1994) From map to model: the development of an urban information system. *Design Studies*, 15(3), 310–36.

8. Anonymous (1994) VR: the quay to success. *CAD User*, 7(9).

9. There will be a great many ways of realizing the objectives set out in the plan. A document can accommodate only a selection, often only one, which can then become, often unintentionally, the 'standard solution'. This is the common problem of the design guide.

CONCLUSION

It has been argued that design control, the process by which public agencies seek to modify the design of development in the public interest, is an essential feature of contemporary government. It is expected by the public in most developed countries and constitutes a political reality that is most unlikely to go away. It is concerned with the quality of the physical environment, urban and rural, in its broadest sense. The fabric of town and country is in the charge of a multiplicity of agencies and is subject to continual modification over time. It is these incremental changes that design control must be effective in guiding and it must guide them according to policies approved through the political system. The problem is that rarely are such policies clearly stated and articulated, particularly outside of town centres and prominent historic areas. This causes great inconvenience to both potential developers and the general public and is inimical to effective design control. Although there are a number of possible explanations for this omission, the one that has been addressed in this book is the difficulty of producing such policy statements in the absence of the type of the extensive methodology that exists, for example, for strategic planning. The task has been to develop an appropriate and practical method.

Any way forward must recognize that the design and development processes require negotiations between a number of interested parties of which the planning authority is but one. Control must be seen as a sophisticated and complex process that relates directly to the negotiations and in a way that can be understood by all the parties, including lay people and the public at large. To be useful in the negotiations, the control procedures should distinguish clearly between intentions and outcomes. They should also convey their intentions through media that are understandable by

lay people. A four-way split has been recommended whereby a distinction is made between objectives, criteria for their achievement, advisory material on possible ways of achieving them and the legal and administrative procedures to be used in their implementation. Furthermore, the objectives should stem from design goals and both the goals and objectives should be published and be subject to public debate. All this could appear as a design plan.

The design objectives should reveal the deliberate policy of the planning authority and should relate to particular localities. The generation of objectives should be facilitated by the use of design areas. These subdivisions of a plan area would relate to the objectives rather than pre-existing concepts such as land-use allocations. They could encompass entities, such as main roads, whose design has long been neglected because of their use as land-use boundaries. They would also facilitate variations in the intensity of design control from place to place. Moreover they would encouraged planning for mixed uses rather than the segregation of residential land from other facilities. A structure of design areas should cover the whole of a planning authority's area even if the objectives propose only a minimal level of intervention. In practice, objectives could be resolved into categories according to different levels of intervention. These could range from minimal intervention, through height and bulk envelopes, controls on form and style to strict conservation of the existing fabric. Criteria, advisory material and control procedures could be developed for all standard objectives and be included in an overall design plan.

The feasibility of producing a design plan on the lines recommended has been demonstrated by a worked example. The complete approach remains to be tried out but there is much evidence from practice that many authorities are not only being increasingly pushed in this direction by the pressure of land development upon them, but have anticipated aspects of the recommendations and have exploited them with success. The use of residential character areas has been particularly striking, as has the use of design area structures in the context of landscape character policy.

The use of design policy in negotiations has been inhibited by the difficulty that lay people have with the technical means of presentation used by the professionals. This problem could be resolved now by the use of computer visualization. In the long term, multimedia and decision support systems should provide the means of making design plans fully responsive in that people could interact with them directly, testing their own ideas against official policy.

Full-scale practical trials of the ideas set out above are now essential. Only by trying them out in the day-to-day work of a planning office can the recommended procedures be tested and refined. This will be particularly so for the standard forms of objective and the criteria for their achievement. Many variations should be tried out and, over the years, the most robust forms would emerge, having been found useful in practice. It would not, however, be necessary to implement all the ideas simultaneously. Selected combinations of the proposals, as may suit local conditions and provide a means of solving particular problems, could be subject to experiment.

The following combinations and choices are suggested to be used in a progressive sequence or selected according to local judgment:

1. making sure that all design policies are clearly stated and articulated, including those that may have been previously taken for granted;
2. distinguishing between the objectives of each policy and what are really performance criteria or control procedures;
3. linking policy objectives to design goals;
4. providing advisory information on possible ways of achieving the objectives;

5. providing performance criteria for each objective;
6. developing a number of design areas with policies for each;
7. extending design area coverage to the whole of the plan area;
8. proving objectives, performance criteria, advisory information and control procedures for each design area;
9. generating alternative objectives for each design area and seeking the views of the public and/or elected representatives on them;
10. exploring standard forms of objective and ways of expressing both them and their performance criteria;
11. using computer visualization for the expression of the above;
12. using multimedia and decision support systems to convey the above.

It is clear that there is a gap that needs to be filled in the control of design. Policy statements, ultimately design plans, are needed that will reveal the full intentions of planning authorities towards the design of the physical environment and convey them to the public in a form that is intelligible to lay parties. A way of developing such plans has been proposed and the examples described have demonstrated that it would be possible to produce them in practice. The efficiency of computer visualization in communicating these policies has also been demonstrated. What is needed now is not only further debate on these proposals but also for them to be tried out in current practice. It is not necessary for all the proposals to be implemented at once. To make the distinction between goals, objectives, outcomes and procedures would be, in itself, a significant step forward, whether or not the design area technique was applied. This technique should, of course, be experimental with and refined and developed further in the light of experience. It is only testing in practice that can eventually produce the system of design plans that is needed so much.

BIBLIOGRAPHY

Audit Commission for Local Authorities and the NHS for England and Wales (1992) *Building for Quality – A Study of Development Control, Local Government Report No. 7*, London: HMSO.

Banham, R., Barker, P., Hall, P. and Price, C. (1969) Non-plan: an experiment in freedom. *New Society*, 26, 435–43.

Barrett, H. and Phillips, J. (1987) *Suburban Style: the British Home 1840–1960*, London: MacDonald.

Beer, A. (1983) Development control and design quality: Part 2 Attitudes to design. *Town Planning Review*, 54(4), 383–404.

Beer, A. and Booth, P. (1981) *Development Control and Design Quality*, Sheffield: Sheffield Centre for Environmental Research.

Bentley, I., Alcock, A., Murrain, P., McGlynn, S. and Smith, G. (1985) *Responsive Environments: A Manual for Designers*, London: Architectural Press.

Bishop, J. and Davison, I. (1989) *Development Densities: A Discussion Paper*, Amersham: NHBRC and the Housing Research Foundation.

Booth, P. (1983) Development control and design quality: Part 1 Conditions: a useful way of controlling design? *Town Planning Review*, 54(3), 265–84.

Booth, P. (1987) Design control. In M. L. Harrison and R. Mordey (eds), *Planning Control: Philosophies Policy and Practice*, London, Sydney and Wolfeboro NH: Croom Helm.

Burton, I. (1992) Planners in mystery play. *Planning*, 993, 17.

Cambridgeshire County Council (1991) *Cambridgeshire Landscape Guidelines – A Manual for Change*, Cambridge: Cambridgeshire CC in association with Granta Editions.

Chapman, D. and Larkham, P. (1992) *Discovering the Art of Relationship: Urban Design, Aesthetic Control and Design Guidance*, Research Paper No. 9, Faculty of the Built Environment, Birmingham Polytechnic (now the University of Central England).

Countryside Commission (1993) *Design in the Countryside*. Technical Paper CCP418. Cheltenham: Countryside Commission.

Cullingworth, B. (1991) Aesthetics in US planning: from billboards to design control. *Town Planning Review*, 62(4), 399–413.

Dacorum Borough Council (1995) *Residential Area Character Study, Discussion Draft*, Hemel Hempstead: Dacorum BC.

Day, A. (1994) From map to model: the development of an urban information system, *Design Studies*, 15(3), 310–36.

Delafons, J. (1990) *Aesthetic Control: A report on the methods used in the USA to control the design of buildings*. Monograph 41. University of California at Berkeley, Institute of Urban and Regional Development.

Delafons, J. (1991) Design control – the American experience. Report of Proceedings, Town and Country Planning Summer School, 1991. *The Planner*, 77(40), 23–6.

Dept. of Environment (1976) *Design Guidance Survey*, London: DoE.

Dept. of Environment (1980) *Circular 22/80: Development Control Policy and Practice*, London: HMSO, paras 19–20. The guidance was repeated in DoE (1988) *Circular 31/85: Aesthetic Control and Planning Policy Guidance Note 1*, paras 27–9.

Dept. of Environment (1989) *Planning Control in Western Europe*. London: HMSO.

Dept. of Environment (1990) *Time for Design: Monitoring the Initiative*, London, HMSO.

Dept. of Environment (1992a) *Development Plans: A Good Practice Guide*, London: HMSO.

Dept. of Environment (1992b) *Efficient Planning*, London: DoE.

Dept. of Environment (1994) *Historic Buildings and Conservation Areas*, PPG 15, London: HMSO.

Dept. of Environment (NI) (1987) *Queen's Conservation Area*. Belfast: HMSO.

Devon County Council (1992) *Traffic Calming Guide*, Exeter: Devon CC.

English Heritage (1993) *Conservation Area Practice*, London: English Heritage.

Essex County Council (1973) *A Design Guide for Residential Areas*. Chelmsford: Essex CC.

Essex County Council (1980) *A Design Guide for Residential Areas: Highways Standards*, Chelmsford: Essex CC.

Essex County Council (1984) *South Woodham Ferrers: Western Industrial Area Design Brief*, Chelmsford: Essex CC.

Gibson, T. (1991) This neighbourhood plan is different. *District Councils Review*, January, 16–17.

Gould, S. J. (1992) London's unitary development plans: design policy and control. *Urban Design Quarterly*. 44, 11–16.

M. Grant (1993) ISSUE (Interactive Software Systems for the Urban Environment). In U. Fleming and S. Van Wyk (eds), *CAAD Futures '93*, Proceedings of the 5th International Conference on CAAD Futures, Pittsburgh, Amsterdam: Elsevier, pp. 557–564 and M. Grant and I. Paterson (1994) Urban Modelling. In T. Maver and J. Petrie (eds), *The Virtual Studio*, Proceedings of the 12th European Conference on CAAD, Glasgow, pp. 135–139.

Habe, R. (1989) Public design control in American communities: design guidelines/design review. *Town Planning Review*, 60(2), 195–219.

Hall, A. C. (1988) Computer visualisation for design and control. *The Planner*, 74(10), 21–5.

Hall, A. C. (1990a) Design control – a call for a new approach. *The Planner*, 76(39), 14–18.

Hall, A. C. (1990b) Generating design objectives for local areas: a methodology and case study application to Chelmsford, Essex. *Town Planning Review*, 61(3), 287–309.

Hall, A. C. (1990c) *Generation of Objectives for Design Control*. Chelmsford: Anglia College Enterprises.

Hall, A. C. (1992a) *Computer Visualisation: An Investigation of its Application to the Control of Urban Design*, Chelmsford: Anglia Polytechnic.

Hall, A. C. (1992b) Letting the public in on design control. *Town and Country Planning*, 61(3), 83–5.

Hall, A. C. (1993) The use of computer visualisation in planning control: an investigation of its utility in selected examples. *Town Planning Review*, 64(2), 193–212.

Hall, A. C. (1995) Visual reality. *Planning Week*, 3(11), 16–17.

Hall, A. C., King, D. and Woodruffe, M. (1994) The potential of multimedia for urban management. *17th Urban Data Management Symposium*, Helsinki University of Technology, Finland.

Hall, P. (1988) *Cities of Tomorrow*, Oxford: Basil Blackwell.

Hawkins, R. (1993) The planning process: what goes on behind closed doors. *The Architects' Journal*, 24 January, 16–17.

Hawkins, R. and Vigars, P. (1993) *Before and After Planning*. Exhibition Guide.

Hendry, J. *et al.* (1986) *Conservation in Belfast*, Dept. of Architecture and Planning, Belfast: Queen's University.

Hillman, J. (1990) *Planning for Beauty*, London: Royal Fine Art Commission, HMSO.

House of Commons (1985) Command 9571: *Lifting the Burden*, London: HMSO.

Johnson, A. (1991) *Your Victorian House*, Newton Abbott: David & Charles, 2nd edn.

Keeble, L. (1971) *Town Planning at the Crossroads*, London: Estates Gazette.

Leeds City Council (1982) *Residential Design Aid 1, Site Potential*.

London Borough of Richmond (1981) *Environmental Character, District Plan Topic Study Report No. 7*.

London Borough of Richmond (1989) *Barnes Green Study, Conservation Area No. 1*.

Lynch, K. (1960) *The Image of the City*, Cambridge, Mass.: MIT Press.

Mandani-Pour, A., Lally, M., Underwood, G. (1993) *Design Briefs in Planning Practice*, Working Paper 26, Dept. of Town & Country Planning, University of Newcastle-upon-Tyne.

Manser, M. (1991) Barriers to design. *RIBA Journal*, 86, 401–3.

Manser, M. and Adam, R. (1992) Restoration of democracy mooted as architects remodel system. *Planning*, 983, 16–17.

Manser, M. and Adam, R. (1992) Putting planning in better shape, *Planning*, 984, 24–5.

Marshall, J. and Willox, I. (1986) *The Victorian House*, London: Sidgwick & Jackson.

Muthesius, S. (1982) *The English Terrace House*. New Haven and London: Yale University Press.

Newbury District Council with Landscape Design Associates (1993) *District Wide Landscape Assessment – A Summary*. Newbury: Newbury DC and Peterborough: Landscape Design Associates.

Nuffield Foundation (1986) *Town and Country Planning: A report of the committee of inquiry appointed by the Nuffield Foundation*. London: Nuffield Foundation, Chs 1 and 2.

Punter, J. V. (1985) *A History of Aesthetic Control I: The control of the external appearance of development in England and Wales, 1909–1947*, University of Reading, Working papers in Land Management and Development, Environmental Policy No. 2.

Punter, J. V. (1985) *A History of Aesthetic Control II: The control of the external appearance of development in England and Wales, 1947–1985*, University of Reading, Working papers in Land Management and Development, Environmental Policy No. 7.

Punter, J. V. (1986) A history of aesthetic control, part 1 1909–1953. *Town Planning Review*, 57(4), 351–81.

Punter, J. V. (1987) A history of aesthetic control, part 2 1953–1985. *Town Planning Review*, 58(1), 29–62.

Punter, J. V. (1990) The Ten Commandments of architecture and urban design. *The Planner*, 76(39), 10–14.

Punter, J. V., Carmona, M. and Platts, P. (1994) Design policies in development plans. *Urban Design Quarterly*, 51, 11–15.

Reade, E. (1987) *British Town and Country Planning*, Milton Keynes: Open University Press.

Reade, E. (1991/92) The little world of Upper Bangor. *Town and Country Planning*, 1991, 60(11/12), 340–3, 1992, 61(1), 25–7 and 61(2), 44–7.

Rodriguez-Bachiller, A. (1991) Expert systems in planning: an overview. *Planning Practice and Research*, 6(3), 20–5.

Royal Town Planning Institute (1990) *Practice Advice Note No. 8*, London: RTPI.

Royal Town Planning Institute (1993) *The Character of Conservation Areas*. Commissioned Study from Chesterton Consulting and University of Central England. London: RTPI.

Southworth, M. (1989) Theory and practice of contemporary urban design: a review of design plans in the United States. *Town Planning Review*, 60(4), 369–420.

Stones, A. (1992) Revising the Essex Design Guide. *Urban Design Quarterly*, 44, 17–19.

Suffolk County Council (1994) *Suffolk Design Guide for Residential Areas*. Ipswich: Suffolk CC.

Vigars, P. (1993) Before and after shot. *Planning*, 1002, 6–7.

Wakeford, R. (1990) *American Development Control*, London: HMSO.

Wales, HRH the Prince of (1989) *A Vision of Britain: A Personal View of Architecture*, London: Doubleday.

Woodford, G. *et al.* (1976) *The Value of Standards in the External Residential Environment*, DoE Research Report No. 6. London: HMSO.

Statutory development plans cited

Buckinghamshire County Council (1990) *County Structure Plan*, Aylesbury: Buckinghamshire CC.

Chelmsford Borough Council (1977) *East Springfield Planning and Design Brief*, Chelmsford BC.

Chelmsford Borough Council (1985) *Chelmer Village South Design Brief*, Chelmsford: Chelmsford BC.

Chelmsford Borough Council (1993) *Chelmsford Borough Plan Deposit Draft*, Chelmsford BC.

Chiltern District Council (1993) *The Local Plan for Chiltern District*, (except *Chesham Town Centre and Waterside*) and *The Chesham Local Plan*, Amersham: Chiltern DC.

Dacorum Borough Council (1984) *District Plan*, Hemel Hempstead: Dacorum BC.

Dacorum Borough Council (1995) *Dacorum Borough Local Plan*, Hemel Hempstead: Dacorum BC.

Essex County Council (1957) *Development Plan for Metropolitan Essex*, Written Statement and County Map, Chelmsford: Essex CC.

Essex County Council (1995) *Essex Structure Plan: Written Statement*, Approved Second Alteration. Chelmsford: Essex CC.

Hertfordshire County Council (1992) *Hertfordshire County Structure Plan Review*, Hertford: Hertfordshire CC.

London Borough of Redbridge (1994) *Unitary Development Plan*, Ilford: LB of Redbridge.

London Borough of Richmond-upon-Thames (1981) *Environmental Character, District Plan Topic Study Report No. 7*.

London Borough of Richmond-upon-Thames (1985) *District Plan*.

London Borough of Richmond-upon-Thames (1992) *Unitary Development Plan*.

London Borough of Sutton (1978) *Living in Sutton, Report of Studies*.

London Borough of Sutton (1981) *Living in Sutton, Sutton District Plan*.

London Borough of Sutton (1988) *Sutton Local Plan*.

London Borough of Sutton (1994) *Unitary Development Plan Deposit Draft*.

Wycombe District Council (1994) *Wycombe District Local Plan*.

INDEX

Index

Index